READ, WRITE and i

Study Guide

For a Telecourse on
English Composition

Writing the Research Paper

Second Edition

Ray Clines

Produced by
Florida Community College at Jacksonville
Jacksonville, Florida

KENDALL/HUNT PUBLISHING COMPANY
4050 Westmark Drive   Dubuque, Iowa 52002

CONTENTS

LESSON PAGE

PREFACE

Higher education should be available to persons throughout their lifetimes, accommodating those who wish to study part time or return to school later in life. Working adults who are continuing their education amidst the competing responsibilities of their families, their work, and their communities often cannot be served by traditional on-campus classes. The Carnegie Commission on Higher Education has repeatedly pointed out that more flexible and diverse educational programs must be created, especially at the postsecondary level. For those wishing to realize their full potential during every phase of their lives, telecourse learning serves a vital function. It offers the technology to draw otherwise excluded individuals into the educational environment, and it keeps those who are already established in their fields aware of the latest advances in knowledge. *Read, Write and Research* is a timely response to the needs of an increasingly diverse college/university student population.

Each lesson in this study guide is designed to encourage effective study habits by providing an organized sequence of reading/viewing/writing activities. Before watching the video lesson, students read the "Lesson Preview" and "Learning Objectives," which present a concise overview of the telecourse material. "View the Video Program" alerts students as they watch the lesson to especially important features that illustrate the learning objectives. After students have watched the lesson, a "Lesson Review" provides print reinforcement for the video presentation. The "Self Test" allows students to check their learning and offers measurable proof of their mastery of the key concepts. The "Writing Assignments" provide the opportunity for students to apply the concepts of the lesson, emphasizing the importance of student participation in the learning process. The *Faculty Guide* available to instructors offers further teaching suggestions and supplementary exercises.

The making of a telecourse and its accompanying materials is perhaps the most inclusive of collaborative efforts, relying on the expertise of people in a variety of fields: script writers, media professionals, production technicians, advisors, educators, and students. Each has made a contribution to the development of this study guide, but I am especially grateful to Kathy Clower and Barbara Burns who brought my initial rough manuscript into clear definition. I also wish to acknowledge the substantial assistance of Liz Cobb both in the actual development of the text and for her patient support.

Ray Clines
Jacksonville, FL
1991

v

ACKNOWLEDGMENTS

Telecourse Development

Faculty Advisory Board

Joan L. Bearden, M.S.L.S., Librarian
William H. Denson III, M.S., Professor of Communications and Humanities
Paul S. Kleinpoppen, Ph.D., Professor of English
Careta R. Russell, M.Ed., Professor of Communications
Charles D. Smires, M.Ed., Professor of English
Arnold A. Wood, Jr., M.A., Professor of English

Contributing Faculty

Joann D. Carpenter, Ph.D., Professor of History
Patrick M. Commons, M.S., Professor of Physics and Mathematics
Joe A. Davis, M.Ed., Professor of Communications
Carol H. Grimes, M.A.T., Professor of Communications
Linda G. Martin, M.A., Professor of Communications
Jim L. Mayes, Ed.D., Professor of History
Victoria S. Register, M.A.E., Teacher of English
Brenda R. Simmons, Ph.D., Professor of Communications
Claude J. Smith, M.A., Professor of Communications
Paula J. Thompson, Ph.D., Professor of Natural Science

Contributors

Kathleen M. Clower, Producer/Project Director
Carol S. Miner, Provost, Open Campus
Robbie Gordon, Scriptwriter
Mark A. Basse, Chief Videographer/Editor
Elyse M. Brady, Administrative Assistant
Jan Brant, Editing Support

PREFACE TO SECOND EDITION

Several years ago when Florida Community College faculty and staff initially designed the English Composition telecourse, it was written to serve our own telecourse students. Consequently, we utilized exercises and examples from our classroom experience to convey the essential skills and concepts we felt necessary for successful research and argumentative writing.

We discovered that one skill was not emphasized as much in the telecourse experience as it is in the classroom. Hence, we have included a critical thinking component to the second edition of Read, Write, and Research.

We were quite mindful that too many changes would significantly alter the basic text, and would create the need to make substantive changes to the accompanying videotapes. Although revisions to the videotapes will be forth coming for the present, we have used the best technology possible to include the changes relating to critical thinking. It is our hope that with the inclusion of the critical thinking elements along with the two basic tools—the video lesson and the guidebook—students will have a solid foundation for researching and writing a documented paper.

Brenda R. Simmons, Ph.D.

Linda Martin, M.A.

COPYRIGHT ACKNOWLEDGMENTS

INTRODUCTION

Lively and contemporary, **Read, Write and Research** is a new television course developed in response to a widely expressed need for a college course on English Composition beyond the introductory level. Essay writing, writing a research paper, writing across the curriculum, writing for business, and writing about literature are the essential components of this innovative course for students continuing in college and those preparing to enter the work force alike. The fast-paced video programs full of lively and contemporary examples from recognizable real-life situations appeal to students of all ages.

Video clips of timely issues have been included to entice the reluctant student as well as reassure the timid or fearful student that writing is not very different from everyday life. Buying a car, planning a vacation, making out a shopping list, purchasing a TV set, going to a movie and selecting a day care center are a few of the many examples of familiar skills which can be called upon for research. Current issues such as the crisis in day care, the war on drugs, gun control, medical malpractice, children of divorce, attitudes toward AIDS victims, the use of steroids among athletes, and family structure as reflected in TV sitcoms are only some of the timely topics used. **Read, Write and Research** will appeal to traditional and non-traditional students alike.

COURSE OBJECTIVES

The video programs and supplementary print materials of **Read, Write and Research** have been developed to:

➤ Provide students with the skills needed to write a research paper with a well-formulated thesis, proper documentation and a complete list of references

➤ Provide students with step-by-step guidelines for writing a research paper, writing essays, writing across the curriculum, and writing for business

➤ Review skills from introductory English composition courses which are applicable to writing a research paper

➤ Acquaint students with the many library resources available for researching a topic

➤ Introduce students to the benefits of using word processing for writing their research papers

➤ Demonstrate the differences between arguable and nonarguable statements and the importance of using arguable statements in developing strong thesis statements

➤ Prepare students to take an essay exam

➤ Prepare students to write about literature

➤ Introduce critical thinking to the processes of reading and writing

COMPONENT MATERIALS

Video Tapes

Twenty-four half-hour video programs.

Study Guide

The **Read, Write and Research Study Guide** provides students with an organized method for viewing and reviewing each lesson. Designed to help students achieve objectives on a lesson-by-lesson basis, the study guide introduces each program, presents lesson objectives, reviews the material covered, provides a self test and includes writing assignments.

Faculty Guide

The **Faculty Guide** offers suggestions for organizing and teaching the television course on a lesson-by-lesson basis. Various writing assignments are listed as suggestions. Due to the nature of this course, no test manual has been prepared. The underlying assumption in the development of this course is that more instructor/student interaction via student conferences and writing assignments will be required than is typical in other telecourses. Instructors are encouraged to tailor assignments to the special needs and interests of their students.

Textbooks

Read, Write and Research can be used with most introductory and intermediate texts for English composition. Instructors are encouraged to select texts that match their students' needs and interests. Suggested companion texts used in the development of the course include:

The Informed Argument; A Multidisciplinary Reader and Guide, Third Edition (Harcourt Brace Jovanovich, 1992), by Robert K. Miller.

The Harcourt Brace Guide to Documentation, Third Edition (Harcourt Brace College Publishers, 1995), by Kirszner & Mandell.

MLA Guide for Writers of Research Papers, Fourth Edition, 1995 (Modern Language Association of America), by Joseph Gibaldi.

Publication Manual of the American Psychological Association, Fourth Edition, 1994 (American Psychological Association).

Secrets of Successful Writing, Third Edition, (Reference Software International, 1989) by DeWitt H. Scott.

Introducing the Research Paper

✔ Lesson Preview

Every piece of writing requires a writer, a reader and something that is written about—the message or content. Usually one of these elements is emphasized more than the other. By shifting the emphasis from one element to another, different types of writing can be created.

Expressive writing results when descriptions of the personal experiences or feelings of the *writer* are emphasized as in diaries, letters or autobiographies.

Informational writing emphasizes the *content* or *facts* about something, as in technical articles or news stories.

Persuasive writing emphasizes the *reader* and attempts to get him or her to act on something. Persuasive writing depends more on logical reasoning and the collection of evidence to support a particular position as in a newspaper editorial or an argumentative essay.

In this lesson you will learn the differences between these approaches and methods for using them to write an effective paper. One way to decide what to write on a topic is to put yourself in your reader's shoes and ask what your reader wants to know. Defining the needs of your audience automatically suggests an approach, a purpose, even the language and tone of your writing. Is the audience knowledgeable about this subject? Are these people experts? Or, do they know very little about the subject and need to have terms defined for them?

Having a lot to say about a subject makes your task of writing much easier. In this lesson you will learn some brainstorming techniques for generating ideas. By making lists and using cluster diagrams, you can go beyond the obvious and offer your readers something of genuine interest.

Once you have generated worthwhile ideas, you will need to order these ideas into an essay. A well-written paper consists of three major parts: an introduction, a body and a conclusion. In this lesson you will learn what information to include in each of these sections and how each part is constructed. You will also learn to use techniques such as transition, parallelism, subordination and coordination to create more interesting and effective papers.

Learning Objectives

After completing this lesson, you will be able to:

➤ Recognize differences among expressive, informational and persuasive writing and the relationship of each to the reader, writer and content

➤ Identify and define your audience

➤ Generate ideas for a topic using the following techniques:

  • Asking questions (Who? What? Where? When? Why? How?)

  • Making lists

  • Creating cluster diagrams

➤ Organize a paper into three main sections: introduction, body and conclusion

➤ Recognize the use of transitional devices, parallel structure, sentence variety, coordination and subordination in writing effective and interesting papers

✔ View the Video Program

As you view the program, look for words and phrases that can be used to help create smooth sentence and paragraph transitions.

✔ Lesson Review

As shown in the video, written communication requires a writer, a reader and content.

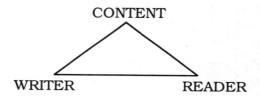

CONTENT

WRITER   READER

A piece of writing usually emphasizes one of these elements more than the other two. Descriptions of personal experiences or feelings of the *writer* produce *expressive* writing, as in diaries, letters, autobiographies and personal opinion essays. As you saw in the program, writing an expressive essay about hot air ballooning included descriptions of how the writer liked her first hot air balloon ride, what clothes she wore, and how she prepared for it. The emphasis was on the *writer.* This type of writing is usually easier because you already know the subject and you are the expert.

When the *content* is most important, *informational* writing results. Examples of writing emphasizing content include scientific and technical articles, textbooks, news stories and articles in encyclopedias. Recall from the video that the student took a historical approach to ballooning to produce an informational essay—how ballooning has developed and changed over the years. Like a news report, this essay was a descriptive account and required outside research.

When a work emphasizes the *reader,* it attempts to get the reader to take some kind of action; it is *persuasive.* Examples of persuasive writing include: advertisements, newspaper editorials and essays. The persuasive essay on ballooning in the video program attempted to convince the reader that ballooning is a very safe sport and one in which people should participate.

Identifying the Audience

The audience is the single most important factor in determining your approach to a topic. Defining the needs of a specific audience will suggest an approach, a purpose, even the language and tone of the writing. As suggested in the program, if you select a birthday card for your sister, you take into consideration the type of person she is. If she has a sense of humor, a card that makes her laugh is good choice. If she's the sentimental type, a flowery type is better. You are considering the reader or audience. The same is true for writing.

By tailoring your message to a specific audience, your writing will be more focused and effective. Ask yourself: Does my audience know a lot or a little about the subject? Are they experts? How old are they? Do they represent a certain segment of the population? What is their educational level? From the program, recall that before writing an essay about using animals for medical experiments, the writer needed to know more about the audience. Was he writing to pet owners, medical students or someone with a terminal illness who could possibly benefit from the research? Different audiences require different approaches.

Exploring Your Topic

The more ideas you have about a subject, the easier your writing task will be. Even before you begin to write, ask the following questions:

Who?   What?   Where?   When?   Why?   How?

Then list everything you can think of that relates to your subject. Recall from the program the list of ideas generated for the topic of paternity leave: effect on career, effect on family, benefits, drawbacks and the reaction of other men. By exploring a subject thoroughly, you can go beyond the obvious and offer your readers something of genuine interest.

Another method suggested for generating ideas was the use of a cluster diagram. Here again it was suggested that the more you write down, the easier and better your writing becomes.

CLUSTER DIAGRAM:

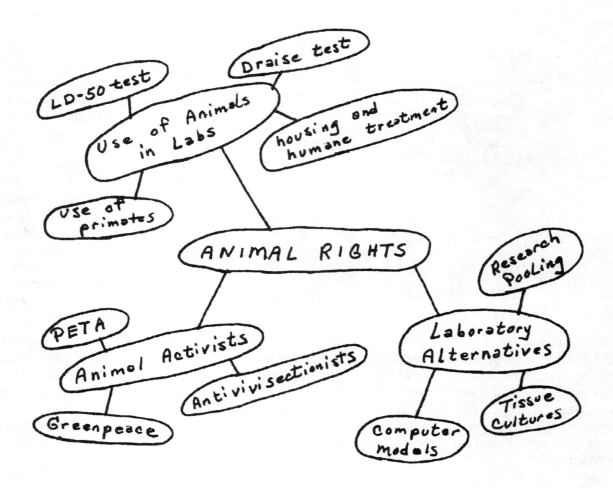

Organizing Your Paper

Once you have generated some worthwhile ideas for your essay, you can begin to organize your ideas into a readable format. An essay consists of an introduction, a body of several paragraphs and a conclusion.

Writing an Introduction

Introductions set forth the general subject and announce the thesis or main point of the paper. A short paper, 500 words for example, requires only a one-paragraph introduction whereas a longer paper can take several paragraphs to introduce your ideas. You can set up an introduction using the form of an inverted pyramid—moving from general information about a topic to the specific focus or thesis of the paper. Recall from the video the introductory paragraph that stated the general subject, appliances, and then focused on the specific subject—the dishwasher.

Writing Body Paragraphs

The body of your paper should address the important topics or issues surrounding the thesis. In the body, which is usually only three or four paragraphs in a short paper, you attempt to explain or prove your thesis. Treat each paragraph like a mini-essay complete with main ideas stated at the beginning, supporting details or examples and a conclusion. The **unity** of an essay depends on all paragraphs in the essay relating back to the main idea and all sentences in a paragraph relating to the central thought in that paragraph.

Because each paragraph deals with a different aspect of your thesis, you should link the paragraphs with **transitions.** You can do this by using words or phrases such as: "for example," "however" or "in addition." You can also repeat key words in all the paragraphs to help bind the essay.

Using **parallel structure** is another way to keep your thoughts unified. Recall the following sentence from the program:

> *I can make do* without my food processor; *I can adapt* when my toaster conks out; *I can manage* without the garbage disposal ....

Notice that each sentence repeats the same kind of phrase and creates a rhythm for the reader.

To hold your readers' attention, you can also vary the length of your sentences. This helps provide sentence variety. Try the techniques of **subordination** and **coordination** to develop longer sentences.

Subordination allows you to show *cause/effect relationships* between your ideas; it indicates which ideas are more important. The program example included two vaguely related sentences that didn't provide the relationship between their ideas:

> I went to Tom's house. His mother was throwing pots and pans at the wall.

The revised, *subordinated* version suggests the main point—Tom's mother was angry—when the first sentence is put into a time relationship.

> *When* I got to Tom's house, his mother was throwing pots and pans at the wall.

Coordination, on the other hand, links clauses of *equal* value by using one of the seven coordinating conjunctions: *and, but, or, for, nor, yet* and *so.* Recall from the video the sentence that linked two equal clauses:

Tom's mother was throwing pots and pans at the wall *and* she was shouting at the dog.

Writing a Conclusion

The final paragraph of your essay should pull together all the ideas you've presented and reach a final conclusion. In longer papers you may need to summarize the main points again. In shorter papers summarizing is not needed and may be repetitive. Either way, your conclusion should leave the reader with a sense of completion or closure. Good writing relies upon seeing beyond the obvious—finding the details most people overlook. Developing observational skills by watching and listening carefully will help sharpen your writing.

Sharpening Your Writing Skills

Throughout your writing, you should demonstrate the development of a more mature writing style. To achieve this level of writing, you should go beyond mere information reporting and start to evaluate, to make judgments and to offer recommendations relating to your reading. You will begin to see the relationship between reading, writing and thinking. When you perfect this interrelationship and become a more thorough writer, you will write from a more mature perspective.

✔ Self Test

From the following list, identify the term that matches the statement. Place the correct response in the space provided.

coordination	sentence variety
expressive writing	subordination
informative writing	thesis
parallel structure	transitions
persuasive writing	unity

1. Writing that emphasizes the author's personal thoughts, feelings or experiences

   _____

2. Writing that emphasizes the facts or content

   _____

3. Writing that emphasizes the reader's point of view and tries to change it

   _____

4. A one-sentence statement in the introduction that expresses the main point of an essay

   _____

5. The relevance of all sentences in a paragraph to the single topic of the paragraph

   _____

6. Also, consequently, finally, further, for example, in addition, in brief, in other words

   _____

7. In any sentence, units of meaning that are equally important and expressed in word groups that are equal in structure

   _____

8. Using different sentence lengths and patterns for interesting writing

   _____

9. In sentence structure, a technique used to indicate the relative importance of ideas and to show specific relationships between them

_____

10. Using the following words to connect ideas of equal importance: and, or, nor, but, for, so, yet

_____

Check your answers at the end of this lesson.

Writing Assignments

1. Write three brief essays of two or three paragraphs on the topic of minority rights. In each essay emphasize one of the following: (a) the reader, (b) the writer or (c) the content. Be prepared to explain the differences and the ways you developed each essay.

2. Using the topic of animal use for medical experiments, write three persuasive paragraphs, each to a different audience: (a) to biology or medical students, (b) to the family member of a person with an incurable disease and (c) to a member of an animal rights organization.

Answer Key

1. expressive writing
2. informative writing
3. persuasive writing
4. thesis
5. unity
6. transitions
7. parallel structure
8. sentence variety
9. subordination
10. coordination

L E S S O N 2

Learning to Use the Library

✔ Lesson Preview

You have probably used library catalogs many times for locating books, but conducting college-level research requires a working knowledge of reference books, indexes, bibliographies, and computer databases as well. Without this knowledge, you will be unable to find important articles in newspapers and journals, or locate essays in collections and anthologies. This lesson will introduce you to these necessary tools for conducting research and explain other services which libraries offer. You will see that a library is more than a building filled with books; it is a true resource and learning center.

Learning Objectives

After completing this lesson, you will be able to:

- ▶ Distinguish between circulating and non-circulating materials

- ▶ Use various catalogs for locating source materials

- ▶ Use the Library of Congress or Dewey Decimal classification system to locate print and non-print materials on a topic

- ▶ Use different indexes, both general and specialized, to locate articles in periodicals

- ▶ Converse knowledgeably with your reference librarian regarding computer searches and the possible use of interlibrary loan

✔ View the Video Program

As you view the program, identify at least three different sources you can use to begin your library research.

✔ Lesson Review

Library materials are broadly classified into three categories: print, non-print, and electronic. Print materials include circulating books that may be taken out of the library and non-circulating reference books, such as encyclopedias, atlases, bibliographies and indexes, that must remain in the library. Examples of non-print materials include microfilm, microfiche, records, audio and video tapes, films and compact disks. Electronic materials include the information available through computers.

Books

Libraries use one of two systems to organize books: the Library of Congress classification system or the Dewey Decimal system. Most college libraries use the Library of Congress classification system. The call numbers in the Library of Congress system begin with one or two letters (PS478.R27, for example) whereas the call numbers for the Dewey Decimal system begin with numbers (973.7.R27, for example). Finding a book by either classification is simple, however. Follow the letters or numbers in order, just as you do for house numbers, to locate the aisle, row, and shelf containing the material.

The Library of Congress system groups books by a single subject. For example, "G" includes all general geography books; "GA" designates mathematical and astronomical geography books; and "GB" represents books on physical geography. In the Dewey Decimal system, however, the three digit number represents the general category (800 for literature, for example) which can be subdivided into more specific categories: 810=American literature, 820=English literature, 821=English poetry, and so on. Many public libraries use the Dewey Decimal system.

Although most libraries are shifting from card catalogs to microfiche or computer systems, the process of locating a book remains much the same: look up your reference by title, author or subject. Electronic or computer catalogs have step-by-step instructions to guide you in their use; if you need additional help, a librarian can assist you.

Locating Your Subject Within a Book

If the catalog doesn't list an entire book on your subject, you may find a chapter *within* a book devoted to your topic. Recall from the video that when a book on the Hindenburg disaster could not be found, a book about great disasters of the twentieth century containing a chapter on the Hindenburg was used instead. An index that will help you find parts of books such as chapters or separate essays is the *Essay and General Literature Index*.

The *Essay and General Literature Index* was used by the student in the program researching art censorship. By using this reference he was able to locate an essay entitled, "The Pleasures of Looking: the Attorney General's Commission on Pornography Versus Visual Images" in the book, *The Critical Image*. With the help of the librarian he was able to determine whether the reference was available in his library and whether it would be relevant to his paper.

Periodicals

Research doesn't end when you have an armful of books—you can also find a lot of material in articles in magazines, journals and newspapers. One major advantage of using periodicals is their currency. Whereas books take many months and even years to be written, purchased and shelved, periodicals can be as current as this morning's newspaper. Because events change so rapidly, articles have replaced books as the primary way of publishing up-to-date information. Furthermore, since an article in a periodical usually focuses on a specific topic, its title often indicates exactly what that topic is, saving you time in your search for relevant sources.

Unlike books, there is not one central catalog for periodicals. Different types of periodicals are indexed in different reference books. There are three main types of periodicals: newspapers, general magazines and professional journals.

Finding Magazine and Journal Articles

As an index to articles in magazines, the *Readers' Guide to Periodical Literature*, is a good place to begin. It indexes general periodicals such as *National Geographic, Rolling Stone, Reader's Digest, Newsweek, Ebony*, and *Sports Illustrated. The Readers' Guide* does not index by title and has limited access by author, so you may find the *Readers' Guide* most useful when researching by subject. Each year's listings contain only those articles written in that year, so you may have to check other volumes for your subject. Recall from the video that while only one article was found on Hell's Angels in the 1984 volume, over three references were found in the 1985 volume. Electronic indexes for periodicals such as *InfoTrac* and *Wilsondisc* are also available. In some libraries you may be able to search periodical databases on-line as well.

Because magazines are written for the general public, they do not usually include technical articles and may oversimplify and occasionally distort some of the ideas presented. For this reason you should continue your research by looking at the more specialized, professional journals. To look up specialized topics, consult indexes such as the *Art Index, Education Index, Biography Index* or the *Criminal Justice Periodical Index* for more scholarly articles. Many of these indexes are also available on computer.

Once you have found article titles in the indexes, you should find out if your library subscribes to the periodicals in which the articles appear. Locate the periodicals list, available either in a separate catalog or in a bound pamphlet in the periodicals section of the library.

Finding Newspaper Articles

Newspapers are valuable sources on almost any subject. All **major** newspapers publish indexes. For example, most libraries carry *The New York Times Index* or *Wall Street Journal Index;* their annual volumes provide information on locating articles often stored on microfilm or microfiche. To find articles from **local** newspapers, you may find *NewsBank* a helpful resource. As you saw in the video, to find information on "Operation Grouper," a drug smuggling sting in South Florida, the student searched the *NewsBank Index* since it was unlikely that the story made national news. After searching by year and subject, articles about the sting were found on microfiche.

Using Interlibrary Loan

If your library does not carry the book or periodical you need, check with your librarian about the possibility of using the interlibrary loan service. Interlibrary loans put the resources of libraries all around the country at your fingertips. The interlibrary loan ser-

vice supplements a library's resources by allowing libraries to borrow from one another. A similar service is provided by database computer facilities. Most information contained in book indexes is now available through databases.

Locating Non-print Materials

You can also find non-print materials such as records, tapes, or films in much the same way you find print materials. Don't overlook non-print materials when researching a topic. They contain much useful information. Consult the library catalog for a complete listing of your library's audio-visual materials.

Beginning Your Search for Information

While all of this information may seem a little bewildering, library research really falls into three general areas: using reference works to define your topic; using catalogs and indexes to find the titles of books and articles; and actually locating the books and magazines on the shelves, on microform, or through interlibrary loan. You may want to begin your search for information with general reference materials like an encyclopedia or a subject encyclopedia. Another good initial source is the library catalog. You can gain valuable information from the catalog entry or computerized record itself. As you saw in the video, the *Readers' Guide to Periodical Literature* was used to find general articles in *Ms.* and *Newsweek* about the topic of abortion. However, to find articles on the psychological effects of abortion, a specialized index such as *Psychological Abstracts* had to be used.

It's easy to see why libraries are called "storehouses of knowledge" and "information centers." Every possible format for recording information is available here. Because there are so many different indexes and retrieval systems in modern libraries, you should introduce yourself to the reference librarian and describe your project briefly. Librarians can tell you about any special resources the library offers and assist you with your research. Remember, the most important resource in the library is the librarian.

Critical Reading

As you engage in the initial reading of your resources and later when you read for a more specific purpose, you should focus on particular points for critical reading. Look at the general structure of the writing. Ask yourself the questions which point to the writer's tone as well as the writer's assumptions. Consider the writer's voice and the overall generalizations made in the writing. When you review these aspects of the writing, you will answer critical questions about the writer's attitude, assumptions and personality. Further, you will be able to evaluate the effectiveness of the selection as a whole.

✔ Self Test

From the following list, identify the term that matches the definition or question and write the correct term on the blank line below the question.

computer search	*Essay and General Literature Index*
Humanities Index	interlibrary loan
Library of Congress	microfilm
The New York Times Index	NewsBank
periodicals list	*Readers' Guide to Periodical Literature*

1. If the call number of a book is PS3503.R2736, which classification does the library use?

   _____

2. A reference source that indexes articles in popular magazines

   _____

3. A list containing the titles of magazines which can be found in your library

   _____

4. A reference source that indexes essays

   _____

5. A reference work that indexes articles on history in scholarly journals

   _____

6. A piece of film used to store information

   _____

7. A good place to look for newspaper articles of national interest

   _____

8. A valuable service if your library doesn't have the book or periodical you need

   _____

9. A good place to look for newspaper articles of local interest

   _____

10. An electronic service that accesses indexed information

Writing Assignments

Library Work

1. Summarize the news events recorded on the front page of one national and two local newspapers for the day your were born. Include the name of the newspapers and the date.

2. Use the *Social Sciences Index* to find a topic in psychology that interests you. Locate and read one of the articles listed. Write a one-page summary of the article.

Answer Key

1. Library of Congress
2. *Readers' Guide to Periodical Literature*
3. periodicals list
4. *Essay and General Literature Index*
5. *Humanities Index*
6. microfilm
7. *The New York Times Index*
8. interlibrary loan
9. *NewsBank Index*
10. computer search

Writing the Research Paper

Selecting and Narrowing a Subject

✔ Lesson Preview

Even though most students say that writing a research paper is something they would rather not do, research for a paper is really no different from research you have been doing all your life. Everything from buying a car to planning a vacation involves research. When you research a subject, your purpose is to find out as much about the topic as you can, and then draw some conclusions based on *your own thinking* and the information you have gathered. The nine steps to writing a research paper include:

1. Selecting a subject
2. Narrowing a subject
3. Preparing a list of sources
4. Forming a thesis
5. Taking notes
6. Developing an outline
7. Writing a first draft
8. Revising the draft
9. Writing the final draft

This lesson explains steps one and two in the nine steps to writing a research paper: selecting and narrowing a subject.

In selecting a subject, you should follow your own interests. Even if the subject is assigned, your focus for the subject should be guided by what you find important or interesting. Not every topic that you may be interested in researching is equally appropriate, however. Begin with what interests you, but then be willing to change or adapt your subject to the resources available and to the length of the assignment.

You should begin research by completing a preliminary search of the books, articles, pamphlets, videotapes, and resource persons that are available. As you scan the resources, ask yourself the following questions:

Who?	When?
What?	Why?
Where?	How?

Answering these questions will help you focus on the subject and provide an overview of the information. As your research progresses, you should remain open to different ways of approaching your topic and even to the possibility of changing it.

Learning Objectives

After completing this lesson, you will be able to:

➤ Recognize the nine steps to writing a research paper

➤ Conduct rudimentary research by gathering information and sifting through your information to arrive at a conclusion

➤ Analyze, explain and comment on the ideas of others

➤ Select a subject to research guided by your interests, the resources available and the length of the assignment

➤ Narrow a subject by reviewing the available resources and then focusing on one particular aspect

✔ View the Video Program

As you view the program, look for the techniques the students used to narrow the focus for their topics.

✔ Lesson Review

As you have seen, you already carry out most of the steps in writing a research paper in your everyday life—whether it's buying a car, planning a vacation or writing a memo to your boss. The process of writing a research paper involves gathering your information, sifting through that information and then communicating your findings in writing.

> **THE FIRST STEP IN WRITING A RESEARCH PAPER IS TO IDENTIFY A TOPIC THAT TRULY INTERESTS YOU.**

The first step in beginning a research project is finding a topic that interests you. Many times in college you will be expected to conduct research on predetermined topics. Even here, your line of inquiry can and should be guided by your personal interests. If you interest yourself, you are more likely to interest your readers. If you are having difficulty deciding on a topic, consider the following:

- What is going on in world events that you would like to know more about? Scan a newspaper or news magazine or watch the evening news for ideas.

- Is there something from your work experience you would like to explore? For example, do you know of a case of age discrimination or sexual harassment?

- What special interests or leisure activities would you like to know more about? Are there safety issues involved? What about investment possibilities?

- What "hot" topics have come up in conversations with friends, in class or on TV talk shows?

Many students have difficulty with a research project because of misconceptions regarding the requirements to complete the task. Some common misconceptions identified in the program include:

Misconception: *One source of information is enough.*

Program example: Arriving at a conclusion based on one source is like walking into a room blindfolded and describing that room based on the information gathered from touching one wall.

Remedy: Gather as many sources as available.

Misconception: *A research paper consists of a series of quotations from various sources linked together with transitional phrases.*

Program example:
On Religion

In spite of all our knowledge about the world, we are not convinced that any of it has any real meaning.

"We know too much, and are convinced of too little."

T. S. Eliot

Religion has no value for people who are starving.

"You can't talk religion to a man with a bodily hunger in his eyes.

George Bernard Shaw

Religion is nothing but a drug.

"Religion is the opiate of the masses."

Karl Marx

As Jonathan Swift said, "We have just enough religion to make us hate, but not enough to make us love one another."

"We have just enough religion to make us hate, but not enough to love one another."

Jonathan Swift

Remedy: Include commentary with your quotations.

The video program illustrated two case studies of beginning research projects. In the first example, students were asked to write about a well-known person who has had a significant effect on society. One student began the research by looking into a topic of personal interest—movies. Although she wanted to do her paper about the man who wrote the script for *The Graduate*, she was unable to find enough resources. In the process of doing her preliminary research, however, she became interested in the star of the movie, Dustin Hoffman, so she decided to change her topic and write about him. Here she faced a different problem—too many resources. At this point it became necessary for her to narrow her subject to some single, manageable aspect of Dustin Hoffman's work and its effect on society.

> **THE SECOND STEP IN WRITING A RESEARCH PAPER IS TO NARROW THE FOCUS OF SUBJECT.**

In the second case study, students were asked to write a paper on some positive aspect of their community. Because of a career interest in medicine, one student decided to research the medical services. Here we saw how the process of researching and narrow-

ing a topic go hand-in-hand. Based on the information that the student gathered in his preliminary research, he was able to narrow his subject to the trauma center of a single hospital.

When writing a research paper, it is necessary to have:

1. A workable subject

2. A personal interest in the subject

3. Adequate supporting material

4. A topic that fits the length of the assignment

> REMEMBER: REMAIN FLEXIBLE ABOUT YOUR CHOICE OF TOPIC. THE PROCESS OF SELECTING AND NARROWING A TOPIC SHOULD BE ON-GOING, SUBJECT TO REVISION ANY STEP ALONG THE WAY.

Critical Thinking and Selecting a Subject

When you select a topic that appeals to your interests and experiences, consider the key issues involved. In addition to the overview questions (who, what, when, where, how and why), ask yourself about the claims the writer is making and look for specific evidence. You will find issues which take on more than one form. You may find issues of fact, policy, value or interpretation. You must determine the issues that are most important to you and those that will lend themselves to a more arguable topic of discussion.

✔ Self Test

Mark each statement True or False.

1. _____ For short papers a single secondary source is often sufficient.

2. _____ If you choose a topic you cannot pursue because of lack of available resources, you have wasted precious time.

3. _____ Although research is important, the most significant part of any research paper is the writer's own analysis.

4. _____ Researching an assigned topic is difficult because you cannot explore areas of interest.

5. _____ Whenever possible, select a subject about which little has been written. The more obscure the subject, the more your instructor will be impressed.

6. _____ When you use an index such as the *Readers' Guide to Periodical Literature*, you should start with issues that were published at least five years ago and work forward to the present.

7. _____ You can narrow a subject in order to make it fit the assigned length of the paper.

8. _____ First-hand information that you obtain through interviews should not be used because it is not as reliable or impressive as information from well-known published sources.

9. _____ Once you choose a subject, you should stay with it until you have found what you need.

10. _____ Ask questions during preliminary research in order to focus on what is really important.

Check your answers at the end of this lesson.

Writing Assignments

1. One of the points in the lesson is that you do research in your everyday life, only you probably haven't thought about it as "research." Now that you are more familiar with the steps in conducting research, think about a time in your life in which you researched a topic that was not a school assignment (such as deciding on a new sound system or deciding what you were going to do on spring break). Write a paragraph or two in which you discuss the following:

   a. What was the purpose of your research?

   b. What sources did you consult?

c.   What steps did you take?

d.   Describe the results of your research.

2.   Choose one of the following general subjects:

Feminism	X-ray Dangers
Nova Scotia	Florida Keys
The Incas	Mental Illness
The Automobile	Education
Divorce	Alcoholism

Go to the library and conduct preliminary research. Based on what you find, narrow the subject so that it would be appropriate for a 700-800 word paper. In a few paragraphs, note the steps you followed, the sources you consulted, and the reasons for narrowing the subject.

Answer Key

1. F
2. F
3. T
4. F
5. F
6. F
7. T
8. F
9. F
10. T

L E S S O N   4

Writing the Research Paper

Preparing a Working Bibliography; Stating the Thesis

✔ Lesson Preview

Preparing a bibliography for a research paper is not very different from preparing a list of estimates for having your house painted, listing estimates for getting your car repaired or compiling a list of day-care centers for your child. In deciding on a day-care center, for example, you would collect the same kind of information on each center you call—the location, the cost, the hours of operation, the size of the staff, teacher-child ratio, etc. A list like this provides the kind of information you need to make a good decision about which center to use. Doing research on an academic subject accomplishes the same purpose: it gives you information from a variety of sources which allows you to draw reasonable and well-informed conclusions about your subject. An important step in conducting research, then, is compiling a list of possible resources.

This lesson covers steps three and four in the nine steps to writing a research paper:

3. Preparing a list of sources

4. Forming a thesis

In this lesson you will be introduced to three categories of research; overview, focusing and supporting materials. You will be shown the differences between primary and secondary resources for research and will learn some of the advantages of using 3 x 5 index cards for keeping track of your information. This lesson will also present five steps to follow for writing a preliminary thesis.

Learning Objectives

After completing this lesson, you will be able to:

► Identify three categories of research materials: overview, focusing and supporting materials

► Describe the differences between primary and secondary resource materials

► Recognize the correct MLA (Modern Language Association) format for noting reference materials

23

➤ Prepare a preliminary bibliography note card

➤ Develop a preliminary thesis statement following the suggested criteria

✔ View the Video Program

As you view the program, look for some of the advantages of using 3 x 5 index cards to compile your bibliography. Note the information you should include for each type of reference.

✔ Lesson Review

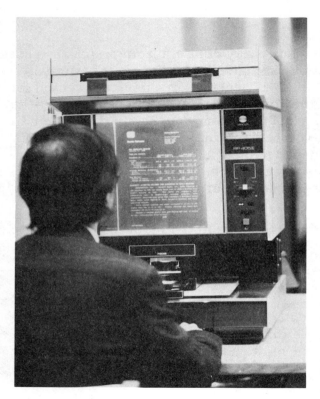

As you have learned, preparing a bibliography for a research paper is no different from collecting a list of estimates for having your house painted or finding the best day-care center for your child. Doing research on an academic subject accomplishes the same purpose—it gives you information from a variety of sources and allows you to draw well-informed conclusions about your subject.

Classifying Research Material

Research can be categorized into three general classifications: overview, focusing and support materials.

Overview Materials

Overview materials, such as encyclopedias, biographies and almanacs, are used as guides to help you *frame* your search. These materials provide general overview information, key words, subject-specific terminology and relevant dates necessary to begin your project.

Focusing Materials

Focusing materials are indexes and reference works that help you *focus* your research on those sources you want to investigate. Focusing materials include various catalogs, such as the *Readers' Guide to Periodical Literature*, the *Education Index* and *The New York Times Index*. Also included in this category are more specialized dictionaries and encyclopedias like the *Encyclopedia of Psychology* and the *Dictionary of American History* that you will need in special cases. As you saw in the program, when looking for information on a prominent, local business person not nationally known, the student didn't find the *Readers' Guide* very helpful. In this case, the student had to use more specialized indexes such as the *Business Periodical Index*, *Who's Who in Finance and Industry* or *The Wall Street Journal Index*.

Supporting Materials

Supporting materials consist of the specific articles, books, essays, written interviews, correspondence and audio-visual materials which provide the information you need to *support* the thesis of your paper.

There are of two types of resources: primary and secondary. **Primary resources** consist of books, articles and other materials written by the actual researcher. If you are writing a paper on the poetry of Robert Frost, for example, Frost's books of poetry are considered primary sources. For a paper on "The Declaration of Independence" the document itself is the primary source. **Secondary resources**, on the other hand, include anything written *about* the subject by another person. Critical works *about* Frost's poetry are secondary sources as well as essays *about* "The Declaration of Independence." To take another example, if you are writing about the work of Sigmund Freud, a book written *by* Freud is a primary source and a book written *about* Freud or his theories is a secondary source.

An often overlooked resource is the personal interview. Talking to experts—doctors, professors, and public officials—through an arranged interview is a good way to add authenticity as well as current information to your paper.

Preparing a Preliminary Bibliography

The first step in beginning a research project, of course, is finding a subject which interests you. Once you have a topic, the next step is to get an overview of the subject before committing yourself to it. Begin by looking through the overview materials. Depending on the topic, you may want to browse through articles in popular magazines or you may start with general encyclopedias such as the *Encyclopaedia Britannica* or *World Book* and then use the library catalog to locate more specialized references such as the *Encyclopedia of World Art* or *Encyclopedia of the Third World*. By using key words from your general references, you can identify subject headings.

Before going too far with your investigation, you should begin preparing a preliminary or working bibliography with 3 x 5 index cards. As you move on to your focusing materials, you can make a bibliography card for each book or article. You will find cards easy to handle and rearrange.

To prepare a card for a book, record the following information:

➤ Name of author, last name first

➤ Title of book (underlined)

➤ Place of publication

➤ Publisher's name

➤ Date of publication

➤ Library call number

For articles in journals or newspapers, include:

- ➤ Name of author
- ➤ Title of article (in quotation marks)
- ➤ Title of periodical (underlined)
- ➤ Volume number/date of publication
- ➤ Page numbers
- ➤ Reference information that will help you locate it again

Figure 1: Bibliography Card for a Book

Figure 2: Bibliography Card for an Article

Note: These cards follow the MLA guidelines for documentation. Ask your instructor about the preferred guidelines for your course.

In the video program, a number of steps were demonstrated for researching the topic and preparing a preliminary bibliography on photojournalism. After consulting an encyclopedia and dictionary, the student checked reference indexes for key terms, such as *photography* and *journalism*. Early pioneers in the field were identified as well. Armed with a number of synonyms for photojournalism and names of past and current photojournalists, the student then began to look for articles in popular magazines using the *Readers' Guide to Periodical Literature*. But for articles on photojournalism as a profession, the student used *Business NewsBank* and the *Business Periodical Index*. For articles on the impact of visual images, the *Social Sciences and Humanities Index* and the *Psychological* or *Sociology Abstracts* were suggested. The following information was noted on an index card:

Figure 3: Bibliography Card

Although personal interviews are an excellent source of information, securing a personal interview for primary research is sometimes difficult. However, don't overlook video tapes and TV programs to find supporting material. The format for the bibliography card is similar to one for articles and books—list the program writer or host first, the name of the program, the production company or network and date of broadcast.

This preliminary listing of materials has a single purpose: to determine whether or not you have gathered enough information to support the ideas for your paper. Look through your preliminary bibliography. If you find that you have ample material, you can begin reading through the books and articles. Your next step is to formulate a preliminary thesis.

Writing a Thesis

The thesis is a single sentence that clearly states the position you take on your topic. Although your thesis may change as you do more reading and accumulate more information, it is important to have a thesis statement developed to give shape and direction to your research. Because your thesis guides your investigation, you should write it with care.

Criteria for Writing a Thesis Statement

1. State your thesis in a single declarative statement, not a question. In the program the question,

    > Do skateboarders pose a hazard to pedestrians?

    was changed to a statement,

    > Skateboarders pose a hazard to pedestrians when they recklessly per form stunts on sidewalks and streets.

2. Make sure you take a position about your subject—that it is an arguable point. In essence, every thesis statement contains two parts: a topic and the writer's idea or position *about* the topic. Recall this statement from the program:

    > Every morning when the paper plant blows its stacks, a foul odor results.

27

The statement is not arguable. It was altered to read:

>   The foul emissions caused by paper plants blowing their stacks are slowly killing and injuring the people of the city.

3. Base your statement on solid reasoning or evidence—not on insupportable personal opinion. If nothing in your preliminary reading seems to support the position you want to take, you can either change your topic or alter your position to reflect current research. As you saw in the program, the statement, "Sunbathing is obscene," is a personal opinion reflecting the writer's bias and should not be used as a thesis statement.

4. State your thesis in strong, specific language. Avoid vague or abstract words such as *interesting, nice* or *good*. Statements such as "Drugs are dangerous," "Players of professional sports are paid too much money" or "Computers are changing our society" say very little because they are too broad. As shown in the video, the following sentence lacks precision:

>   The large sums of money to be made from dealing drugs creates an interesting problem for communities.

The sentence was revised to read:

>   The gold jewelry and expensive cars which drug dealers flaunt attract even children to this illegal billion-dollar industry.

You should remember that critical writing does not mean finding fault. It means that you make an informed assessment of your topic.

Additional Examples

>   Neutral statement:
>
>   Thousands of people are killed each year in highway accidents.
>
>   Position statement:
>
>   Stricter drunken driving laws must be passed to reduce the number of people killed each year in highway accidents.
>
>   Neutral statement:
>
>   Studies have shown that room colors affect people's moods.
>
>   Position statement:
>
>   Schools, hospitals and prisons should be painted in appropriate colors to affect people's moods.

5. Make sure your thesis statement presents a manageable objective that fits the length and scope of your assignment. Trying to cover all aspects of the fast-

food industry or the field of photojournalism, for example, would require hundreds of pages.

This thesis is too broad:

> The fast-food industry is an ideal business.

In order to limit the thesis, the thesis was rewritten:

> The fast-food industry appeals to those who want to invest in businesses where the demand for their product will always exist.

It is better to limit your topic and treat it in-depth than to select a broad subject and deal with it superficially.

Recall the steps the student followed in formulating a thesis for the topic *photojournalism*. After reading articles and taking notes, she developed the following ideas: ethics and photojournalism, economic aspects of photojournalism, the effects of innovations and technology on photojournalism, and war photography. Her preliminary thesis combined two of her ideas, but was too vague:

> Photojournalists record the tragedy of war so that they can elicit sympathy from the public.

The thesis was edited for preciseness, but then became too wordy:

> Because they are attracted to the tragedies of war, photojournalists try to capture the intensity and pain of battles without regard to their subjects or their subjects' families.

The thesis was revised to read:

> Laying ethics aside, photojournalists capture the agony and intensity of victims of war.

With a manageable thesis and a working bibliography, you are now ready to move on to the next step—taking notes.

✔ Self Test

For each pair of sentences below, place a check next to the sentence that qualifies as an arguable thesis statement.

1. _____ a. On the average, people with college degrees will have lifetime earnings which are nearly double those without degrees.

   _____ b. Although earning power may be more, a college degree does not necessarily ensure a graduate a better life.

2. _____ a. Advances in medicine and longer life expectancy have not altered Americans' fear of dying.

   _____ b. Because of medical advancements, the life expectancy of Americans has risen steadily over the past 100 years.

3. _____ a. Watching spectator sports has become the most popular pastime of the American public.

   _____ b. For many Americans watching spectator sports has taken the place of religion.

4. _____ a. The English language is gaining supremacy in world politics.

   _____ b. English is the most widely used language in the world.

5. _____ a. FCC regulations limit profanity and nudity on major network television programs but not on cable networks.

   _____ b. The only way to prevent questionable television programming is through government censorship.

Indicate the type of research material—overview, focusing or supporting—on the blank line below the question.

6. *Twentieth Century Authors: A Biographical Dictionary of Modern Literature*

   _____

7. An article entitled "Psychoanalysis and Education" in *The Atlantic Monthly*

   _____

8. A college textbook entitled *Introductory Psychology*

   _____

9. An article entitled "Psychoanalysis" in *The Encyclopaedia Britannica*

   _____

10. *Oxford Economic Atlas of the World*

_____

11. A book entitled *Franklin Bibliography: A List of Books Written by, or Relating to, Benjamin Franklin*

_____

12. The library catalog

_____

13. A book entitled *Concepts of Psychoanalysis*

_____

14. An essay entitled "Ideology and State Apparatuses" in the book *Lenin and Philosophy and Other Essays*

_____

15. A book entitled *Freud and His Theories*

_____

Check your answers at the end of this lesson.

Writing Assignments

1. Select one of the following topics to research. Use your library to compile a working bibliography of ten sources that are available in your library. Following the steps in this lesson, use overview, focusing and supporting materials. Quickly read through some of the sources you find and write a preliminary thesis statement for a five-page paper. Make sure your thesis fulfills the criteria mentioned in the lesson.

   Suggested topics:

Biracial Adoption	Homeopathy
Rap Music	Single Sex Education
Tennis	Juvenile Court
Law Enforcement	Halloween
Sunspots	Acupuncture
Whales	Terrorism

2. Describe the steps of your research in the previous assignment. Indicate which overview materials, e.g., *Encyclopedia Americana*, and which focusing

materials, e.g., *Bibliographic Index: A Cumulative Bibliography of Bibliographies* you used. Discuss any problems you had locating articles and which resources you found most useful.

Answer Key

1. b
2. a
3. b
4. a
5. b
6. overview
7. supporting
8. overview
9. overview
10. overview
11. focusing
12. focusing
13. supporting
14. supporting
15. supporting

L E S S O N 5

Writing the Research Paper

Taking Notes

✔ Lesson Preview

Critical
Reading
and the
three R's:
A Key
to Making
Judgments

When you select a special section of the newspaper to read or decide to watch one TV program instead of another, you are making decisions based on what you think will be the most informative, the most useful or perhaps the most interesting. You are evaluating your choices and making judgments. Selecting materials for your research paper is done in much the same way. You select sources and collect information based on what you think is important for your research. You may find that some materials are more valuable than others just as you may discover the TV program you have selected is not as good as you had expected it to be. In this lesson you will learn how to judge the sources for your research paper by using the "three R's": Relevance, Recency and Ranking. You will learn to evaluate your sources by asking:

Is this material relevant to my research?

Is the information current?

Of all the sources I have collected, which is most important? Which is least important?

In this lesson you will be presented with tips and techniques for taking notes. You will learn the difference between a fact and an opinion and you will see that by carefully considering the content of your sources, you can avoid arriving at false conclusions. Good note-taking skills can help keep you focused on your project, aid you in organizing your material and help you avoid plagiarism. By following the suggestions in this lesson, you learn that the task of taking notes is really a manageable process.

Learning Objectives

After completing this lesson, you will be able to:

► Judge the usefulness of your sources using the three R's: Relevance, Recency and Ranking

► Use direct quotes, paraphrase, summarize and extract key terms from a source for your notes

► Distinguish between fact and opinion in your sources

► Identify the main points in your sources

► Avoid plagiarism

✔ View the Video Program

As you view the program, look for time-saving tips on taking notes. Try to identify those that will be most useful to you.

✔ Lesson Review

As you saw in the video, research is a process with which you are already familiar. Whether you are seeking statistics on your favorite team or looking for a new dessert recipe, you probably consult many different sources. Conducting research for a paper is very similar. You go to a variety of sources for the information you seek. In the beginning stages of your project, it is sometimes difficult to determine what type of information is most valuable.

Judging Your Sources

You can evaluate each source using the "three R's": Relevance, Recency, and Ranking.

Relevance: Is the source relevant to your thesis?

You can determine the relevance of your source by first examining the table of contents, the index, the preface or the introduction of a work. Or you may want to skim an article to see if it touches on the main points of your paper's idea before beginning serious reading. The program presented a thesis concerning the long-term effects of divorce on children. Clearly an article on how to find a good divorce lawyer was not relevant, but an article addressing the idea that divorcing parents are often too concerned about their own problems to notice those of their children did fit the central idea.

Recency: Is your information current?

Unless you are writing from a historical standpoint, you should try to use the most current information available. Newspaper and journal articles usually provide more recent information than books. When you do use a book as a source, remember to check the publication date. In the program example, information published before the Roe vs. Wade decision in 1973 was found to be outdated and could not be used in the student's paper on abortion. Older references can be used, however if you want to make historical comparisons.

Ranking: Which of your sources are most important?

Ranking is the process of listing sources according to their importance—from the most to the least important. To determine ranking, you should consider a number of factors: Who wrote the material? What are the author's credentials? Is the material based on fact or opinion? What is the purpose of the article? Rely on those articles and books which most closely relate to your thesis. If you are writing on the role of human intervention in wildlife preservation, for example, you may find an encyclopedia article on the habitats of the grizzly bear to be less important than a recent newspaper article describing the success of relocating grizzly bears to higher mountainous areas. When writing an essay on air pollution, the student in the program was presented with two very different pieces of information: a pamphlet generated by a local company, a major polluter, and a newspaper article written by a reputable reporter. Although both sources were relevant to the thesis and provided pertinent information, the intent of the pamphlet was found to be in question. The pamphlet, therefore, was considered a less reliable source of information and received a lower ranking in importance.

Taking Notes

In order to manage all of the information you are collecting, you need to:

➤ Condense the information by finding the main ideas in each source

➤ Evaluate each piece of information

➤ Jot down the information on an index card

This is the process of *note-taking.*

To make note-taking easier, use index cards and follow these suggestions:

1. Allow only one idea per card.

2. Write only on one side of the card.

3. List the source and page number for each reference on the card.

4. Label each card with a brief description of what the note is about, using headings that relate to your outline.

5. Write a full note so that weeks later you will be able to understand what you wrote.

6. Do not throw anything away.

7. Keep your working bibliography cards handy when taking notes so that you can identify your sources.

8. Read over the last set of cards to refresh your memory before beginning a new note-taking session.

The important point here is that you learn to develop a system which ensures that you attribute the ideas from your reading to the appropriate authors.

> **Keeping track of ideas on note cards will help you categorize your information and organize your ideas. Early systematization will also help you see the natural organization of your paper.**

An important consideration in the process of taking notes is deciding whether to quote directly, paraphrase, summarize or record only key terms and phrases from your sources.

The Direct Quote

Use direct quotes when you want to include those ideas expressed so precisely that you cannot improve upon them or condense them without sacrificing meaning. The appropriate use of direct quotations can add emphasis, emotion and logic to your argument. Recall the impact of the direct quote in the video program.

Remember to cite the author, title and page number of the source for the quotation.

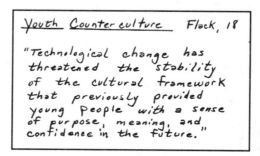

Youth Counter culture   Flack, 18

"Technological change has threatened the stability of the cultural framework that previously provided young people with a sense of purpose, meaning, and confidence in the future."

Figure 1: Direct Quote Note Card

Caution: Use direct quotes sparingly. Too many direct quotes can cause you to lose credibility— as well as the interest of your readers.

Paraphrasing

When you paraphrase, you rephrase the author's ideas by putting them into your own words. Paraphrasing is one of the most important note-taking skills you can learn. Paraphrasing helps you think critically and make judgments about your topic. In the video program you saw the description of the X-29 test aircraft was simplified, yet the original meaning was retained.

Full Quotation:

All three of these surfaces are tied into a digital computer and their deflection or movement during flight is optimized by the flight control computers. When the pilot makes a stick input to the airplane, these three surfaces all react simultaneously to give you optimum response to the airplane to minimize drag and maximize performance.

Paraphrase:

Digital computers connected to the surface of the airplane wings monitor the movement and provide that information to the pilot. This allows the pilot to make immediate adjustments and helps improve the plane's performance.

As with the direct quote, remember to acknowledge the source of the paraphrase by noting the author, title and page number.

Caution: You may be tempted to color the paraphrase with your own opinions or evaluations. Be aware of your biases and avoid inserting your own opinions in the paraphrase. Be sure you do not misrepresent the author's ideas.

Summarizing

Summarizing allows you to condense large amounts of information into as few sentences as necessary. When you summarize, try to capture only the general idea from a passage. The video program presented information about the X-29 aircraft and then condensed it into one sentence:

Computers connected to the wings help the pilot improve the performance of airplanes.

Youth Counterculture   Flack 1-19

Author argues that prior to 1960 social scientists viewed Am. culture as very stable.
In recent decades technological change has rendered traditional practices and institutions irrelevant. Counterculture groups and student movements developed.

Figure 2: Summary Note Card

Note: You can often find summary information in an introduction or a first chapter.

Using Key Terms

Key term notes can be used for recording important phrases and words which may be helpful later. Recall from the program the information about the X-29 aircraft was further condensed by using key phrases:

flight control computers
optimum response
minimize drag
maximize performance

Again, remember to record the author, title and page number of the source on your note cards.

Youth Counterculture   Flack 1-19

Generation Gap
Student Activism
Political Dissent
Radicalism
Cultural Crisis
Authoritarianism

Figure 3: Key Terms Note Card

Avoiding Plagiarism

Plagiarism is using someone's ideas or words as if they were your own. In order to avoid plagiarism you must document everything you use from outside sources. Don't be tempted to skip over the details of documentation to make your writing go more quickly. If you forget to credit a source, even unintentionally, you are guilty of plagiarism. Remember that both non-print and print materials are protected by copyright laws. You may not use someone else's ideas as if they were your own.

Distinguishing Between Fact and Opinion

Distinguishing between fact and opinion is another important note-taking skill. A fact is information which can be verified, whereas opinion offers information which cannot be proved.

Fact:

Humane Society officers found five puppies in a dumpster in LaFayette Park today.

This statement can be proved. If true, it is a fact.

Opinion:

The five puppies found in the park dumpster today were most likely left there by teenagers who usually have no respect for animals.

This statement is purely conjecture or a guess about who left the animals. This statement reflects the writer's bias; it is an opinion.

Be aware that editorials and book and movie reviews contain more opinion than fact; however, many articles contain both. You may use both opinions and facts to support your thesis, but you must distinguish between these types of information for your reader.

Recall from the video program:

Fact:

In 1989, more than four thousand people in the United Stated died of AIDS.

Opinion:

People who get AIDS deserve what they get.

Fact or *Opinion*?

Demi Moore is considered one of the finest actresses of our time.

Although this statement can be perceived as an opinion, movie reviews from reputable sources may provide information to document this claim.

Avoiding Incorrect Conclusions

In the program Cuba was described as a perfect tourist spot complete with casinos and sandy beaches. You soon learned that the source book citing this information was outdated and should not have been used. Cuba cannot be considered a great tourist spot today. This example was used to illustrate the importance of checking publication dates before making inferences and drawing conclusions.

A nutrition pamphlet published in 1945 may recommend eating a lot of beef and eggs to maintain health, but a nutrition pamphlet today would recommend fish and whole-wheat bread products. Readers would question your credibility if you used the 1945 pamphlet as your primary source and recommend large amounts of beef and eggs for a good diet. Make sure you have *enough* information and that you have used *current* data before you draw conclusions.

Identifying the Main Idea

Determining the main idea of your source will help you make better use of that source when writing your paper. Before taking an inordinate amount of notes, read over your sources and try to extract the main idea from each. Skimming the material a second time will provide an even better overview. You may want to try summarizing what you have read in one sentence before writing down anything else. From the program, recall the article about envisioning your future and how that can affect success. A number of different main ideas were suggested—from losing weight to performing math problems. You can see how the main point of an article can be easily overlooked at first.

Remember: Document everything you use from outside sources.

✔ Self Test

Mark each statement True or False.

1. _____ To save time, you should have pen and paper handy and start taking notes as soon as you begin reading your sources.

2. _____ The relevance of a source is measured by its authoritativeness.

3. _____ Newly published books are the best source of recent information.

4. _____ When you are ranking sources, you should rank the more technical articles and books as most important.

5. _____ The author, title and date of publication for the source should be recorded on each note card.

6. _____ A paraphrase records the ideas from a source in condensed form.

7. _____ Direct quotes add credibility and should be used often.

8. _____ Paraphrasing is the most important note-taking skill you can develop.

9. _____ When you paraphrase, it is not necessary to change every word in the original.

10. _____ It is usually safe to assume that if something is in print, it is a fact.

11. _____ Identifying the central or main idea of an article is useful only when summarizing.

12. _____ Jumping to conclusions can occur if you rely on too few sources.

13. _____ You should use note cards to jot down the important information in abbreviated form.

14. _____ You should use note cards rather than sheets of paper for taking notes because cards are more easily shuffled and rearranged.

15. _____ As you write summaries and paraphrases, you should include your reactions and opinions.

Check your answers at the end of this lesson.

Writing Assignments

1. Read the following passage written by Catherine Belits (from the article, "Environmental Protection Ordinances Help Farmland Preservation" published in *Small Town* in October 1989).

   The alarming rate of development of farmland into residential subdivisions has created an increasing interest in farmland preservation throughout the Boston-Washington, D.C. metropolitan corridor. Municipalities are searching for ways of keeping as much as possible of the countryside open and in a viable agricultural lifestyle while still absorbing development. Some rural communities have the unique opportunity to avert the destruction of the very environment that has lured those seeking rest from the crush of nearby metropolitan areas. (12)

Using three 3 x 5 note cards make: (a) a summary note card of the entire passage, (b) a quotation note card of the first sentence, and (c) a paraphrase note card of the second sentence. Remember to include information necessary for documentation and easy identification.

2. Find an article or book of interest and prepare the following:
   1. A bibliography note card
   2. A summary note card
   3. A paraphrase note card
   4. A direct quote note card
   5. A key terms note card

Answer Key

1. F
2. F
3. F
4. F
5. F
6. F
7. F
8. T
9. T
10. F
11. F
12. T
13. F
14. T
15. F

L E S S O N 6

Preparing a Working Outline

✔ Lesson Preview

Critical Thinking drives the logic of outline.

Just as an architect develops a blueprint for building a house, you should prepare an outline before writing your research paper. In the past you may have scribbled a few notes to yourself before starting to write, but when you undertake a major writing project such as a research paper, you must have a plan from which to work. This written plan is your outline.

> **An outline for writing a paper is like a blueprint for building a house.**

Although it is difficult to plan a paper completely in advance of actually writing the first draft, an outline will help you order your main points and guide your note card arrangement. Sometimes the brief descriptions or headings on your note cards can be grouped together; these groupings may become the main points of your outline and paper. At other times a logical order for presenting your ideas may not be so readily apparent and another approach will be required.

In this lesson you will learn to develop an outline from using different methods such as the "kitchen sink" approach. You will learn how to gather ideas that relate to your preliminary thesis, identify relationships among the ideas, and selectively choose the most convincing and significant points for your paper. You will also learn that your thesis may be too broad or too narrow and that fine-tuning may be necessary. You will learn how to alter your thesis due to newly discovered information, conflicting viewpoints, lack of supporting material or too much information. This is step six of the nine steps to writing a research paper.

Learning Objectives

After completing this lesson, you will be able to:

➤ Recognize the difference between a phrase (topical) outline and a sentence outline

➤ Begin an outline using one of several methods presented

➤ Use the "kitchen sink" approach as a method of selecting random ideas in order to develop a topic

- ➤ Use note card headings to develop the main points in a topical outline

- ➤ Restate or alter your thesis to fit your outline and ideas

- ➤ Order and unify topical ideas in your outline to support your thesis

✔ View the Video Program

As you view the program, try to identify the thesis statements that the example outlines support.

✔ Lesson Review

As you have seen in the program, developing an outline can be a manageable process. Your note cards help guide the direction of your outline, just as your outline guides the development of your paper. Any large project requires a plan from start to finish.

When first reviewing your note cards, a logical order may not be clear. If this is the case, you can try the "kitchen sink" approach. Without worrying about the order of the items, try to get down as many ideas as you can that relate to your topic. You will probably have more ideas than you can use; don't worry, you can be selective and choose the most convincing and significant points for your paper later. Once you have a fairly complete list, you can begin looking for relationships among the various ideas.

Creating an Outline

The first step in creating an outline is looking for relationships among your ideas and choosing the most convincing and important points. From the video program, recall this example:

Thesis:

> Lotteries attract many people who normally wouldn't gamble but who are willing to spend a few dollars for the possibility of a great return.

Using the "kitchen sink" approach, the student generated a preliminary list of ideas:

- ➤ Big winners seen on the news

- ➤ State governments using lottery money for public programs

- ➤ Large amounts of money spent on advertising and promotion

When the student examined this list more closely, she realized that the last two ideas didn't really relate to her thesis.

Revising the Outline

Sometimes it is necessary to restate or revise the main ideas in your outline so they reflect the focus of your thesis.

Since the **allure** of the lottery was really the main point of the student's thesis, she revised her outline and generated a new list of ideas. After a great deal of thought she came up with a different list:

- ► Sample ads
- ► Big winners on the news
- ► Targeting specific audiences
- ► Cost of lottery tickets
- ► Views of advertising executives
- ► Money spent on advertising/promotion
- ► Lottery terminals in stores

The problem with this outline is that all of the subheadings relate to only one main idea: marketing and persuasive techniques. Since outlines should consist of several main points and include the minor points related to each, the outline needed additional revisions.

The second step in creating an outline is arranging your points in logical order.

Begin your list with the most important points and continue listing them in descending order. As you include specific information from your notes, your outline becomes more detailed. A detailed outline saves you much time and work as you begin organizing and writing the first draft.

Check to be sure you're using the correct form: Roman numerals for main points, capital letters for subheadings, numbers for minor ideas, and lower case letters for any supporting details.

 I. Main Point
  A. Subheading
   1. Ideas under subheading
    a. Supporting detail
    b. Supporting detail
   2. Idea
  B. Subheading

  Remember: An outline must contain at least two items or categories in order to be listed.

Revising the Thesis

You may discover your preliminary thesis is too broad or too narrow and that you need to restate the controlling idea of your paper. Several circumstances may occur which may cause you to alter your thesis.

Topic Too Broad

If your topic is too broad, it will produce an unmanageable amount of information. As you saw in the program, the thesis on TV sitcoms was originally too broad and had to be narrowed and fine-tuned several times. Ask specific questions to discover related, but more manageable ideas. What factors are involved? What examples can you include? In the program example, the original thesis was rewritten to include only four major headings.

Revised thesis:

The portrayal of the family in TV sitcoms reflects changes in American society. Major headings:

   I.   Traditional or nuclear families

   II. Single-parent families

   III. Blended families

   IV. Dual-career families

Topic Too Narrow

If your thesis is too limited in scope, you may not have a sufficient number of main points to raise. Recall from the program that there were not enough points to support the topic of employee morale and cocaine use on the job. The thesis was expanded to include financial liabilities to the employer. The revised thesis yielded several more main points.

Fine-tuning the Thesis

Although not listed as an official step in the writing process, *fine-tuning* your thesis will undoubtedly be a necessary step somewhere along the way.

New Facts or Information

You may discover new facts or information which affect your position. In the example on cholesterol, the working thesis had to be changed when the student discovered that both good and bad cholesterol exist. In light of the new information, the thesis was altered.

Original thesis:

Americans should change their diets to minimize their intake of cholesterol.

Revised thesis:

Although recent research has shown some cholesterol to be good, most Americans should lower their intake of bad cholesterol.

Disagreement Between Sources

You may discover that your sources do not agree. Disagreement among sources occurs primarily when you are dealing with a controversial issue. In the video example, an equal number of qualified sources were found for and against mandatory lie detector tests for employees. In this case choose the side about which you feel more strongly.

You may discover information that disagrees with your original thesis. If this is the case, don't change the position you are taking in your thesis—simply acknowledge the new information. For example:

Original thesis:

> Employers who require workers to take lie detector tests are invading their employees' privacy.

Revised thesis:

> Although employers need to guard against theft and substance abuse by their employees, lie detector tests are an invasion of privacy and should not be used.

Lack of Supporting Evidence

Lack of supporting evidence for your thesis can be due to research not yet released, use of outdated information, or a topic that is too narrow. Recall the example about hyperactivity as a result of a milk product allergy.

Original thesis:

> Parents who want to control hyperactivity in their children should avoid giving them milk products.

The writer could not find enough information to support the cause and effect relationship she was trying to establish. She revised her thesis.

Revised thesis:

> Parents concerned about hyperactivity should consider food allergies as a possible cause.

Too Much Information

Some subjects yield too much information for a single researcher to read. Recall the example on cocaine addiction. When the student entered the term "cocaine" into the computer, he was overwhelmed with the number of entries. The term was too broad, so he refined his search.

Original thesis:

> Cocaine addiction is a critical problem in communities across America.

Revised thesis:

> Cocaine addiction in the work place costs the employer and eventually the public, millions of dollars a year.

Fine-tuning your thesis is often a necessary step somewhere along the way. Approach the outline process with the understanding that your thesis is unproved and, therefore, may not be entirely valid. Your thesis may have to be amended many times in the course of your research. Each bit of new information forces you to ask if your thesis is still on target and if it is stated precisely enough to guide the direction of your paper.

✔ Self Test

Mark each statement True or False.

1. _____ Once you have read through your resources and notes, you should have a pretty clear idea of the direction of your paper and the kinds of information needed to back up your thesis.

2. _____ Since many questions may occur to you as you think through your topic, use those questions in your outline.

3. _____ Note card headings can be used as main points of an outline.

4. _____ The "kitchen sink" approach works best when a logical order is not immediately apparent.

5. _____ Your final detailed outline should include most of the information you have collected, including ideas only indirectly related to your thesis.

6. _____ Your final thesis is often different from your working thesis.

7. _____ Discovering new or previously unknown facts is likely to occur as you read through your sources and take notes.

8. _____ Conflicting opinions can be integrated into your paper, but conflicting facts are best left unacknowledged.

9. _____ If you can't find enough supporting material for your thesis, you should find a new topic.

10. _____ An overabundance of material for your paper means that your thesis is not sufficiently narrowed.

Check your answers at the end of this lesson.

Writing Assignments

1. For each of the following, write a paragraph of several sentences:

   a. Explain the uses of an outline. Describe some of the difficulties you may run into as you develop your outline.

   b. Describe several ways a working thesis may change.

2. If you have not written a formal outline before, you may want to practice on a piece of writing that is already organized logically. Choose a magazine article of two or three pages and outline it using the following form: Roman numerals for the main points, capital letters for the subheadings, numbers for any minor ideas under each subheading, and lower case letters for any supporting details.

   As an alternative to the above assignment, try outlining a chapter from one of your textbooks.

Answer Key

1. T
2. F
3. T
4. T
5. F
6. T
7. T
8. F
9. F
10. T

L E S S O N 7

Writing the Argumentative Essay

✔ Lesson Preview

Writing an argumentative essay involves many processes you already know and use. It also requires critical thinking and writing skills. Whenever you hear or read something you have an opinion about—whether it's on TV, in the newspaper, or in personal conversation—you probably have the beginning of an argumentative essay. Arguments can be used to convince your friend that you need to borrow his car, get an extension on a term paper, convince an employer that you deserve a raise or to try to talk the police officer out of giving you a ticket.

Writing an argumentative essay is a lot like taking one side of an issue on a talk show. You must take a position on some issue and make a claim. A claim is simply the position which you are defending. Obviously, some things are not arguable. In this lesson you will learn to tell the difference between a statement that is arguable and one that is not. You will learn how to change a nonarguable statement into an arguable one. And you will learn how to write a good arguable thesis.

Learning Objectives

After completing this lesson, you will be able to:

- ➤ Determine the difference between an arguable and a nonarguable statement
- ➤ Change a nonarguable statement into an arguable one
- ➤ Address the appropriate reader/audience in argumentative writing
- ➤ Establish credibility and persuade your readers by:
  - Demonstrating your knowledge of a subject
  - Establishing a common ground with the reader
  - Demonstrating fairness to opposing viewpoints
- ➤ Use deductive and/or inductive reasoning to support your thesis
- ➤ Avoid logical fallacies

✔ View the Video Program

As you view the program, look for the differences between *arguable* and *nonarguable* statements.

✔ Lesson Review

As you have seen in the program, a thesis lays out the claim that will be proven in the essay. Thesis statements can be claims of fact, claims of value, or claims of policy.

Claims of fact argue that something is or is not. Facts are anything that is verifiable. While many facts are not arguable, our grasp of facts is constantly changing based on new research and discoveries. For instance, currently paleoanthropologists disagree whether Lucy, a skeleton more than three million years old, is the common ancestor of human beings. Yet, continued discoveries and more sophisticated techniques promise to decide the debate. When arguing claims of fact, you must be careful to use reliable statistics.

Critical Thinking determines the content of the claim

Claims of value are judgment statements. They approve or disapprove. Value claims contain judging words such as right, wrong, beautiful, ugly, fair or unfair. Values are defended or attacked by referring to a recognized standard or criterion. When arguing claims of values, it is essential that you are very clear about the standard you use to judge since it becomes the premise, or assumption, on which you base your argument. An example of a claim of value is to argue that employers have a moral obligation to provide health insurance for their employees.

Claims of policy advocate an action to be taken. Essays typically follow a problem/solution format. Almost always *should* or *must* is contained in the thesis. "The university must increase its course offerings for evening students" is an example of a claim of policy. In supporting claims of policy, precise definition is necessary. In addition, using facts and value statements will also be persuasive.

> **THE FIRST STEP IN WRITING AN ARGUMENTATIVE ESSAY IS TO MAKE SURE THAT YOUR THESIS STATEMENT IS TRULY ARGUABLE.**

Nonarguable statement:

In recent years greater numbers of children under school age have not been inoculated against communicable diseases.

Arguable statement:

All children should receive the standard series of inoculations against communicable diseases.

COMMUNICATION TRIANGLE:

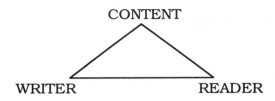

Emphasizing one element of the triangle over another will produce a different type of writing

Emphasizing the writer produces expressive writing.

Emphasizing the content produces informational writing.

Emphasizing the reader produces argumentative/persuasive writing.

Of all types of writing, argumentative writing is the most dependent upon your reader or audience. Good argumentative writing has the potential for the greatest impact on the reader.

An argumentative essay attempts to convince readers of an idea, change their minds about an issue, or urge them to take action. For this reason it is vital that you understand your audience.

> **Knowing whom you're trying to convince will help you frame your argument and decide which points to emphasize.**

In order to persuade your reader to accept your point of view, you must ESTABLISH CREDIBILITY. You can do this in three ways: by demonstrating your knowledge of the subject, by establishing a common ground, and by demonstrating fairness to the opposing side.

> **TO ESTABLISH CREDIBILITY**
>
> **Demonstrate Your Knowledge**
>
> **Establish a Common Ground**
>
> **Show Fairness to the Other Side**

Critical Thinking drives the choice of evidence

Demonstrating knowledge of the subject means convincing your readers that you are thoroughly familiar with the important issues that relate to your topic. Supporting your points with careful explanations, relevant examples, reliable statistics and authoritative testimony is the best way to show that your opinions are knowledgeable.

Establishing a common ground means finding those areas of your subject where both sides are in agreement. For example, regardless of whether you are for or against mandatory drug testing in the workplace, everyone agrees that drug-related accidents should be minimized.

Demonstrating fairness to the opposing side means anticipating opposing arguments and giving them a sympathetic interpretation. In the example of gun control, the writer acknowledged that guns do not *cause* crimes or violent behavior:

Guns don't kill people; people kill people.

The writer then used the opposing side to strengthen his argument.

But why allow guns to become part of the equation? It only makes the outcome more deadly....

Critical Thinking determines the tone of the argument

One more technique to employ when writing argumentative essays is choosing words that persuade. Frequently these words are connotative, or emotionally loaded words. These words convey the tone, or attitude, of the essay. Selecting persuasive words is complicated because you are not always completely sure of the position of your readers. Most likely, readers will hold many varying views. So you must convince those who are in agree-

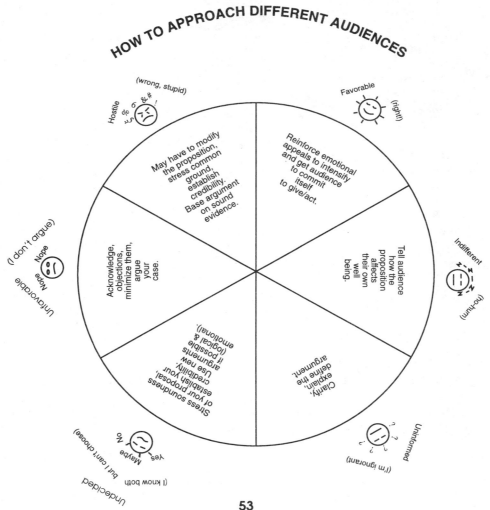

HOW TO APPROACH DIFFERENT AUDIENCES

Hostile (wrong, stupid)

Favorable (right!)

Indifferent (no-hum)

Uninformed (I'm ignorant)

Undecided (I know both but I can't choose)

Unfavorable (I don't argue)

May have to modify the proposition, stress common ground; establish credibility. Base argument on sound evidence.

Reinforce emotional appeals to intensify and get audience to commit itself to give/act.

Tell audience how the proposition affects their own well being.

Clarify, explain, define the argument.

Stress soundness of your proposal, establish your credibility. Use new arguments if possible (logical & emotional).

Acknowledge, objections, minimize them, argue your case.

ment, those who don't know, those who don't care, and those who are hostile. Precise word choice can appeal to each of these groups. Remember, your goal is to persuade, not pick a fight.

> **A good argumentative paper is based on an appeal to logic.**

Inductive and Deductive Reasoning

As you begin organizing your evidence, you will use reasoning to tie your evidence to the claim in your thesis. The two classical approaches to logic into which all critical reasoning falls are inductive and deductive.

Inductive Reasoning proceeds from the specifics—the facts, data, specific examples—to reach a conclusion. For example, arguing on the basis of a single visit that a certain restaurant has excellent food is less convincing than reaching the conclusion after five or six visits and after tasting several different meals. Along with examples, statistics are often used in inductive reasoning. When considering statistics, questions you need to satisfy include: is the sample known, is the sample sufficient, and is the sample representative.

Deductive Reasoning as seen in the form of a syllogism constructed by the Greek philosopher, Aristotle, over two thousand years ago, moves to a logical conclusion from a generally accepted assumption. Complete deductive syllogisms are constructed in the following manner:

Major Premise: All real estate representatives who sell one million dollars worth of real estate in one year are invited to join the One Million Club.

Minor Premise: Maria has sold one million dollars worth of real estate in the past year.

Conclusion: Therefore, Maria will be invited to join the One Million Club.

Questions about your deductive conclusions include: is the premise true, is the syllogism valid, and is the language unambiguous.

Avoiding Logical Fallacies

Clear reasoning requires hard work, time and careful attention to detail. Some people want quick answers and easy solutions. For the sake of argument they will jump to conclusions or use shortcuts which actually detract from their positions. There are several logical fallacies or errors to avoid as you frame your argument.

Oversimplification occurs when you fail to investigate an idea thoroughly. Instead of recognizing several causes or effects, oversimplification reduces an event to a single cause or effect. In the video program the author dedicated his book to a woman other than his wife. This action was not proof that he was unfaithful: the other woman could have been his daughter, mother or sister. Other oversimplification errors include *non sequitur* ("it does not follow") which arrives at a conclusion based on false or nonexisting assumptions. "Because Joe spends generously on dates, he will make a good husband" is a statement in which the conclusion does not logically follow the premise. *Post hoc ergo propter hoc* ("after this, therefore, because of this") assumes that just because one event occurred before another, the first caused the second. Because Joe received a lawn mower for his birthday, he will—not necessarily—have the most beautiful lawn on the block. *Circular reasoning* restates the argument itself, with no additional evidence, as a reason for accepting it. For instance, the traffic jam on Main Street is the result of too much traffic. Don't reduce your argument to oversimplified statements.

Personal attack or *name-calling* (*ad hominem*) is an attempt to discredit the opposing view by attacking the person rather than the issue. Not only is personal attack a digression from the main point of an issue, it limits the writer's credibility. Calling someone a "liberal," or a "chauvinist," or a "communist," or a "feminist" will alienate the very people you are trying to persuade.

A similar situation—guilt *by association*—occurs when someone tries to ascribe the actions of a group to an individual member of the group. Not all men are chauvinists, nor do all Republicans believe in the same things.

Using *ambiguous language is* another trap to avoid. Do not use vague terminology and undefined abstractions. Note the italicized words in the following sentences. The terms are almost impossible to define in the context in which they are used.

Coke™ is the *real thing.*

Crime has become a *way of life.*

Kids are *great.*

The successful writer builds an argument slowly and pays careful attention to word choice and concrete evidence. The successful writer is aware that a reasonable tone and solid evidence will result in effective communication.

✔ Self Test

Put a check beside those statements which are arguable:

1. _____ Cigarettes cause serious health risks.

2. _____ Cigarettes should be made illegal.

3. _____ Billboard advertising must be regulated.

4. _____ Billboard advertising has become increasingly popular with advertisers.

5. _____ Most movies contain offensive language.

6. _____ The offensive language contained in movies should not be censored.

7. _____ People should consider keeping their married status single.

8. _____ More people are choosing to remain single than ever before in history.

9. _____ Mandatory seat belt laws should be repealed.

10. _____ Thousands of lives could be saved each year through the use of seat belts.

In the blank at the left, write the name of the logical fallacy each sentence contains:

ambiguous language	personal attack
circular reasoning	non sequitor
guilt by association	post hoc

11. _____ Never trust anyone over thirty.

12. _____ William is the best quarterback this school ever had. He is the highest scorer in our school's history. He'll be the best president of the Student Council.

13. _____ The silent majority is concerned with law and order.

14. _____ As I was walking on the sidewalk of Maple Street, a truck roared by billowing noxious smoke. Within two hours I was feeling nauseated and dizzy. Let someone try to tell me car pollution is not a problem.

15. _____ I'm on a roll. I made an A on my statistics exam, an I on my cultural diversity paper, and an A on my French presentation. There's no doubt in my mind that I'll make an A on Professor Aristotle's fallacy test, whether I study or not.

16. _____ People are idiots if they can't see that destroying the rain forests will destroy the earth's atmosphere.

17. _____ The traffic congestion is a result of there being too much traffic.

18. _____ When the bell rang, the birds began to drop dead. I can't understand how a bell ringing could kill birds like that.

19. ____ He's always guilty of hasty generalizations because he draws generalizations too quickly.

20. ____ I don't like you very much. In fact, I consider you a radical, so don't even try to convince me.

Writing Assignments

1. For each of the arguable statements in questions 1-10, write a sentence or two that express some "common ground" on which both sides could agree. For example:

    Arguable statement: Drugs should be legalized.

    Common ground: Drug addiction is a serious problem.

2. Choose one of the arguable statements in questions 1-10 (or select an arguable statement of your own) and write a one-page essay on each side of the issue (for a total of two pages).

Answer Key

1. nonarguable
2. arguable
3. arguable
4. nonarguable
5. nonarguable
6. arguable
7. arguable
8. nonarguable
9. arguable
10. nonarguable
11. guilt by association
12. non sequitor
13. ambiguous language
14. post hoc
15. non sequitor
16. personal attack
17. circular reasoning
18. post hoc
19. circular reasoning
20. personal attack

L E S S O N 8

Critiquing the Argumentative Essay

✔ Lesson Preview

An argumentative essay attempts to convince readers of something, change their minds about an issue or urge them to take some action. When you write an argumentative essay, you should identify and address your audience, establish your credibility and persuade your readers.

In this lesson you will view a class in session as they review their own essays and attempt to improve them. You will see how they are able to strengthen their thesis statements, how they write to their readers, and how they provide appropriate examples. At the end of this lesson, you will find one of the student essays critiqued in the program and another that takes the process of argumentation one step further.

Learning Objectives

After completing this session, you will be able to:

➤ Recognize weaknesses in your own essay

➤ Improve your own argumentative essay by applying some of the principles reviewed

✔ View the Video Program

As you view the program, look for suggestions for improving the student essays that may apply to your own argumentative essay.

✔ Lesson Review

As you saw in the video, in argumentative writing it is especially important to address the appropriate audience. You should attempt to establish your credibility and persuade your readers by demonstrating your knowledge of the subject, establishing a common ground with the reader, demonstrating fairness to opposing points of view, and choosing persuasive words. Ask yourself these questions: Who is the audience? What is the counter argument? Is the supporting evidence fair and adequate?

Identifying Your Audience

Of all types of writing, argumentative writing is the most dependent upon your readers or audience. Knowing whom you're trying to convince helps you frame your argument and decide which points to emphasize. Who are your readers? What are their beliefs? What points should be addressed?

Consider Rosemary's thesis from her essay, "Should a College Degree be Trimmed in Gold?"

Thesis:

> Experienced and dedicated employees can be a better choice for promotion than an inexperienced employee with a degree.

Rosemary's audience was identified as company executives and/or those persons in charge of hiring. Knowing whom she was trying to persuade was essential for selecting the supporting evidence:

> Hiring a degreed employee from outside can involve many costs: advertising, interviewing, agency fees, training costs and in most cases a higher starting salary.

These examples provide effective support for her thesis because many executives are concerned with keeping company costs low and profits high. In addressing the concerns of the appropriate audience, Rosemary was able to strengthen her position.

Establishing Your Credibility

Critical Thinking evaluates the evidence

To persuade a reader to your point of view, you must establish credibility. Credibility can be established by demonstrating your knowledge about a subject, establishing a common ground with the reader and demonstrating fairness to the other side. Credibility in argumentative writing is best achieved by incorporating information and supporting evidence in the form of direct quotations, paraphrases and summaries from sources of research. Instead of merely expressing your opinion based on your personal knowledge, you are using the strongest possible evidence to convince your audience. In Lesson 10 you will learn how to incorporate your supporting evidence into your essay.

Following Rosemary's essay, in an essay by Silvana titled "Legal Immigration—Help or Hindrance" credibility is established within the introductory paragraph by fairly reflecting the concerns of her opponents. She then states her thesis:

> Regardless of the reservations of some, legal immigration must remain the policy of the United States.

Silvana takes a strong position in her paper. Because she cites research, she appears informed and knowledgeable about her topic.

Writing a Strong Thesis Statement

When you write your thesis, make sure it is arguable—one that is controversial or that can be argued from the other side. You should state your thesis as strongly as possible. The thesis in Silvana's essay was strong and arguable. Her use of the verb *must* added strength to her statement. Examine your own thesis statement carefully to see if it can be improved.

Acknowledging Opposing Views

One way of strengthening your argument is to acknowledge opposing views and then use these points to your advantage.

Critical Thinking assesses the values behind assumptions

Rosemary's essay includes some examples which support the opposing point of view. However, by including the statement, "Hiring a degreed employee from outside can involve many costs: advertising…" she was able to acknowledge the other side and then refute it. In this way she was able to strengthen her argument.

Silvana accounted for opposing views in a more structured way. She voiced each objection as the topic sentence of a paragraph and then used the body of the paragraph to refute the objection. This method demonstrated Silvana's knowledge of her reader's objections, and it also enabled her to develop enough supporting evidence to counter each argument.

Although many elements must be considered when writing an argumentative essay, make sure you identify your audience, establish your credibility with supportive statements and acknowledge opposing views. These techniques will help strengthen your argumentative writing.

Writing Assignments

1. Review your own argumentative essay in light of the information presented in the class. What suggestions would the instructor have had for you? How can you improve your own essay?

2. Choose two of the topics listed below, focus and narrow it, and write a thesis statement containing a policy claim.

   Suggested topics for Argumentative Essays: —

Battered Spouses	Standard English
Casino Gambling	State Militia Movements
Dress Codes	Teaching Phonetics
English Only Movement	Telecommunications Mergers
Genetic Engineering	U.S. Military Intervention
Medical Insurance	Vegetarian Diet
Oil Prices	Violence on Television
Privatizing Prisons	Vitamin Supplements

SHOULD A COLLEGE DEGREE BE TRIMMED IN GOLD?

Job placement in a middle or upper management position has often been reserved for the person with a college degree. A quick glance through the classifieds reflects that most companies have educational standards or requirements. At times, the "BA in business, Masters pre-ferred" is chosen over the years of experience an employee within the company is able to offer. One can argue that the degree holders have exercised stamina and fortitude by achieving this accomplishment. They have a theoretical basis for any business decision that might need to be made and a wealth of knowledge at their disposal. Their inexperience manifests itself as an energetic and "eager to please" candidate. How-ever, an employee who has been working with the same company for an extensive period of time can surely be attributed these same qualities. In addition, he has shown dedication, loyalty and a working functional knowledge of the company's operations. Companies would benefit by rec-ognizing the strength behind motivating their cohesive, productive, working pool by acknowledging the work accomplishments of the indi-vidual through job advancement. Experienced and dedicated employees can be a better choice for promotion than an inexperienced employee with a degree.

Hiring a degreed candidate from the outside can involve many costs: advertising, interviewing, agency fees, training costs and in most cases a higher starting salary. Once an applicant has been selected, the employer still runs the risk that the new employee may not demon-strate or generate the dedication and loyalty necessary for a success-ful leader.

On the other hand, by promoting the established employee, the em-ployer is able to eliminate hiring costs, reduce training expenses, and negotiate on a reasonable augmentation of salary. The risk of unsatis-factory work behavior is reduced as the employer is already familiar and obviously satisfied with the established track record.

The 1990's promise a more candid look at the value of the dedicated and productive worker and how the employer can maintain and encourage these distinctive qualities. As companies begin to realize the signifi-cance of internal company training, stringent educational requirements will become less a priority and the loyal, skilled employee will be afforded the opportunity of growth potential at the work place.

Submitted by Rosemary Jones

LEGAL IMMIGRATION-A HELP OR HINDRANCE

For centuries the United States has offered an open door to people in need all over the world. The open door policy has recently become an ethical issue. Now at the end of the twentieth century, people are becoming skeptical about immigration. Frequently, workers and politicians have laid the blame for many problems on this country's immigration policies. Some people believe that problems such as rising unemployment, falling wages and rising crime are due to the immigration policies applied by the government. Regardless of the reservations of some, legal immigration must remain the policy of the United States.

Those opposed to an open door policy are quick to offer their reasons. Their biggest concern is that immigrants are taking jobs away from the native born and depressing wages. Roger Corner believes that Americans lose jobs because employers hire immigrants who are willing to work for less (251). Others are afraid of the strife the alien newcomers bring about.

Although American citizens are right to be concerned about their future, they need to look objectively at the facts. While a steady stream of newcomers arrives each year, they bring positive results. First of all, immigrants do not take jobs from Americans, but instead, create jobs for them. Julian Simon argues that immigrants take jobs that American workers do not want in industries like restaurants and hotels (248). Immigrants are people who live in this country and contribute to its economy with purchasing power and by paying taxes. By selling more goods and services, business have to hire more people to meet the growing demands (Volgenau & Mitchell, 1H.+).

Another concern is that immigrants are depressing wages since they are willing to work for any wage. However, in 1989, the U.S. Department of Labor studied the situation and concluded that aliens do not affect the earnings of the native born Americans (Volgenau & Mitchell, 1). In contrast, by keeping wages low in some industries, such as textiles, immigrants actually help businesses stay in the U.S. instead of moving overseas. As a result more jobs are generated for U.S. citizens and the cost of goods remains lower (Volgenau & Mitchell, 1H.+). Many farmers interviewed by Garvin Glenn believe that if they did not have the cheap labor of aliens, the cost of produce would rise forty percent since Americans do not accept a minimum wage (18-26). Additionally, Joseph Martino observes, "The immigrant brings with him the job of providing his sustenance, and he brings with him the hands to produce the re-sources he consumes" (257).

Still another reason some people give for limiting immigration is the growing threat of crime and terrorism in the U.S. They believe that foreigners may harbor subversive ideas or turn to gangs and the under-world. Examples cited are the Asian gangs on the West Coast and, of course, the bombing of the World Trade Center in New York City. Robert Kelly argues, "The Asian criminal figures in the U.S. at first came through legal immigration agencies..." (78-80). Kelly adds that these gangs constantly fight over territory and control of gambling, drugs and prostitution (78). On the opposite coast occurred the bombing of the World Trade Center. Some would point out that this act of terrorism was organized by aliens accepted by the U.S.

Although a few immigrants come to the U.S. for a new life and turn to crime, a few people do not speak for many. Americans are too quick to blame the minorities and aliens for everything that goes wrong. A long remembered example is the bombing of the federal building in Oklahoma City. The media immediately published rumors of foreign terrorist involvement. William Woo points out that immigrants received a backlash after the bombing before it was discovered that "domestic interests" were involved in that terrible criminal act (B,1:1). In reality, tens of thousands of immigrants come to this country every year, most of them good people and hard workers. People who have criminal records prior to entering the country can be stopped by the immigration authorities before they arrive here. On the other hand, terrorist groups from around the world will get in somehow if they intend to. Stopping immigration will not assure public safety.

Overall, immigration brings far more good than bad. In a global economy, reflects Keith Henderson, immigrants benefit the U.S. because they speak different languages and know different cultures (11). No other country in the world has that advantage. The benefits of immigration to the growth of the economy and enrichment of our culture can be seen in every community. The commitment of the United States to remain a country of immigrants should be as strong today as ever.

Submitted by Silvana Haxhiu

WORKS CITED

Conner, Roger. "Immigration Lowers the Living Standards of Americans."
    Opposing Viewpoints: America's Economy vol. 1, 1995: 251.

Garvin, Glenn. "The Real World Consequences of Closed Borders." Reason
    Apr. 1995: 18-26.

Henderson, Keith. "The Melting Pot in the 1990's: Immigration as an
    Economic Engine." Christian Science Monitor. 19 Mar. 1992.

Kelly, Robert J. "Organized Crime: Past, Present, and Future." USA To-
    day. May, 1992:11.

Martino, Joseph P. "Immigration Need not be Restricted." Opposing View-
    points: America's Economy vol. 1, 1995: 257.

Simon, Julian. "Immigration Raises the Living Standards of Americans."
    Opposing Viewpoints: America's Economy vol. 1, 1995: 247.

Volgenau, Gerald and Charles Mitchell. "Immigration: Hate and Hope."
    Detroit Free Press. 28 Nov. 1993: 1H+. SIRS Researcher CD-ROM.

Woo, William F. "A Nation No Longer Quite so Indivisible." St. Louis
    Post Dispatch 7 May 1995, sec. B:1.

L E S S O N   9

Composing on the Computer

✔ Lesson Preview

If you have typed papers in the past, you know what a time consuming process composing on a typewriter can be. Using a computer for word processing can save you much time and effort. Writing, revising and correcting are some of the tasks that can be made easier. In short, electronic word processing is an efficient way of recording and correcting information. The concept of word processing is not very different from that of using a pencil. You record information and when you make a mistake, you simply *erase* it. Word processing, however, has the distinct advantage of being faster. Obviously, learning word processing on a computer is more complicated than using a pencil, but as with any new activity, you can improve with practice.

In this lesson you will be introduced to some of the important terms, functions and tasks related to word processing. If you are unfamiliar with or intimidated by technology, this lesson will ease you into the world of computing and help minimize your apprehensions. Although you will not be a word processing expert after this lesson, you will be able to begin practicing word processing with confidence.

Learning Objectives

After completing this lesson, you will be able to:

► Describe the benefits of using word processing for research papers

► Recognize basic computer terminology

► Define the terms *menu, option* and *file*

► Describe the use of the function keys: *escape, delete, return* and *enter*

► Avoid some of the common word processing pitfalls such as losing information and running out of formatted disks

✔ View the Video Program

As you view the program, look for features of different word processing programs which may be useful to you.

67

✔ Lesson Review

As you have learned, word processing is not a new concept; recording and correcting information have been around for a long time. Word processing is now done on a personal computer, or a "P.C." A computer, like your brain, cannot perform a task unless it has been told what to do and how to do it; in other words, it must be programmed.

Computer Basics

All computers work from programs which provide instructions to perform certain tasks. These programs may be installed on the hard drive of the computer or they may be stored on a disk. Disks work a lot like phonograph records except they store information instead of music. Most disks today are encased in a small, rigid covering (three-and-a-half inch disk). As you saw in the video program, you must handle your program disks carefully. Avoid exposing them to extreme heat or cold and magnetic fields.

Also referred to as software, program disks can direct your computer to perform certain functions, such as delete words or lines, move paragraphs, or check spelling and grammar. Like books, computer programs have different titles.

Using Commands and Function Keys

To record information on a disk you must provide *commands* or instructions. Just as you press the record button on your tape recorder, you hit *enter* on your computer to *record* data or information. By giving your computer certain commands, you can perform certain functions such as underline words, center titles, and move entire lines and paragraphs. Most word processing programs contain a mini-lesson or tutorial which teaches you how to use the commands in that program.

Using the Keyboard

As you saw in the video program, a computer keyboard resembles the layout of the keys on a typewriter. The computer keyboard, however, contains additional keys, such as *Esc* or *Escape* and *Del* or *Delete* which perform specific functions. For example, in some programs you can use the *Escape* key if you need to stop what you're doing or if you have selected a wrong command. The *Ctrl* or *Control* key is used in conjunction with other keys to perform special functions such as saving a file or deleting a sentence.

Directional or *arrow* keys move the cursor—the blinking mark that notes your place—up, down, left and right on the screen. In some software programs the arrow keys used in conjunction with other commands can actually move the cursor from the beginning to the end of the document.

The *Delete* key is a quick correction button, deleting one or several letters or lines. Methods for deleting large blocks of information vary from program to program.

The *Enter* or *Return* key performs two functions. Like a typewriter, the *Return* key moves your cursor to the next line. In addition, this key is often used to tell the computer to begin whatever you have commanded it to do. Just as pressing *enter* at the electronic banking machine sends information to the *brain* of the machine and tells it to carry out the transaction, pressing *enter* or *return* on the computer keyboard tells the computer to perform that particular function, such as save a file.

Choosing Options Through Menus

One of the first things you may see on a screen is a *menu,* a list of tasks your computer can perform. Like a dinner menu, your computer menu presents you with choices or *options.* Two important options are *file* and *edit.*

For example, after selecting the *file* option from the menu, a new menu appears:

Open a File (start a new letter or report or open an existing document)

Save a File (record it on your disk or hard drive)

Retrieve a File (pull it from the *electronic filing cabinet*)

Clear a File (remove it from the screen to start a new f1le)

Print a File (print a file on paper)

Each file or electronic folder must be given a name. The name of the file should be short and descriptive so that you can find it again easily. Since each program has its own set of rules for naming files, you should become familiar with the procedures for naming and saving files for your own program.

Checking Your Spelling

The spell-check option can help you proofread your paper by locating misspelled words. Misspelled words are identified and a list of options are presented on the screen. By selecting the preferred word, you can correct the spelling errors in your paper. Some of the more sophisticated programs even identify double occurrences. Recall the program example:

The the software was inoperable.

The student was able to correct the error by deleting one *the.* Spell-checkers, however, cannot check your paper for context. In the program example, while the word *neglect* was highlighted because it was misspelled, the following sentence passed the spell-check test:

To bee ore not too bee, that is the question.

On the other hand, *Mr. Greene* was flagged as misspelled when G-r-e-e-n-e was indeed the correct spelling for his name.

Caution: Because spell-check programs do not *understand* the meaning of your sentences, you must read your paper carefully for context. Spell-check programs do not correct grammar or punctuation.

Writing Papers Using Word Processing

Once you are familiar with some of the computer's functions, you can see how word processing can help you become a better writer. You can begin your paper by writing the first draft longhand—if you are not yet comfortable with composing on the computer—or you can begin by composing your paper on the screen. In either case you can run a *hard copy* or a print-out of your work after you type it and give it a file name. You can revise the hard copy by hand and then make changes on the computer. You do not need to rewrite pages and pages by hand; you can make all of your changes—even major ones, like moving paragraphs—on your computer screen. In addition, if your program contains a spell-check or a grammar-check function, you can even improve the mechanics of your writing. The time you save in using the special features of your computer can then be devoted to the more complex and important issues of generating good ideas, drafting and revising.

Advantages and Disadvantages of Word Processing

Although the advantages of word processing far outweigh the disadvantages, there are a few pitfalls to avoid. The main problem you may encounter is loss of information either by unintentionally erasing it, losing it if the electricity goes out, or damaging or misplacing a disk. To avoid these problems, you should prepare a back-up disk—a second copy of your data or information—and save your text as often as possible. A good rule of thumb is to save every ten minutes or after every paragraph. Every time you change a file you must save it to effect the change. If you do not save changes, your computer will process your material as if it never received your new instructions. Make sure to keep blank formatted disks on hand. You don't want to be caught with a brilliant thought and nowhere to put it!

Finally, be patient in your word processing education. The long-term benefits of using a computer help you forgive the extra time and frustration you may experience in learning the ins and outs of word processing.

✔ Self Test

Match the term with the definition:

hard copy	*enter* or *return*
file	*escape* key
P.C.	spell-check
option	cursor
commands	saving frequently
menu	directional or arrow keys
control key	software

1. An electronic folder for storing information

_____

2. The command that tells the computer to begin carrying out your instructions

_____

3. A display of the array of tasks your computer can perform

_____

4. A safeguard to prevent accidental erasure

_____

5. Specific instructions which are typed or keyed in

_____

6. A general term for computer programs or instructions stored on disks

_____

7. A personal computer

_____

8. The key which may cancel a command or allow you to leave what you are doing

_____

9. The blinking mark on the screen that denotes your place

_____

10. Used in conjunction with other keys, the key which tells the computer to perform specific functions

_____

11. A function listed on a menu

_____

12. The keys which move the cursor up, down, left and right

_____

13. A print-out on paper

_____

14. The program which will not recognize the difference between *to, too* and *two*

_____

Check your answers at the end of this lesson.

Writing Assignments

1. Write at least one page (approximately 250 words) describing your current knowledge of computers and your past experience with them. Include your views on the value of computer literacy in today's world—its benefits and drawbacks.

2. If your experience with word processing has been very limited, locate a computer lab at your school and ask if you may type the above entry. Print a copy to review.

Answer Key

1. file
2. *enter* or *return*
3. menu
4. saving frequently
5. commands
6. software
7. P.C.
8. *escape* key
9. cursor
10. *control* key
11. option
12. directional or arrow keys
13. hard copy
14. spell-check

L E S S O N 10

Writing the First Draft

✔ Lesson Preview

By this time you have spent many hours locating your sources, reading your material, taking notes and developing an outline. You should have narrowed your subject to a workable thesis. Now you are ready to write.

> Organizing your information for your research paper is a little like putting together a jigsaw puzzle. You have all the pieces you need. Now you have to put them in place.

In this lesson you will learn some important points to keep in mind as you write your first draft. You will learn the importance of remaining flexible as you develop your outline so that new information can be included and your points can be reordered. In addition to the function of the outline, you will learn about the use of note cards, transitions, direct quotations, and citation of sources within the text of your first draft. This is step seven of the nine steps to writing a research paper.

Learning Objectives

After completing this lesson, you will be able to:

➤ Organize your notes into an outline

➤ Use the appropriate form to credit your sources in order to avoid plagiarism

➤ Use effective "lead-ins," transitions and explanations to integrate source material

➤ Follow guidelines for using direct quotations

➤ Draft a preliminary introduction and conclusion for your paper

✔ View the Video Program

As you view the program, look for phrases and transitions which are used to connect the ideas presented. Think about transitional devices and "lead-ins" you can use in your own research paper.

✔ Lesson Review

As you have seen, writing a first draft requires much more than simply copying your notes. Without your own perceptions and logic guiding the paper, you have little more than a "cut-and paste" version of other people's ideas.

Before beginning your first draft, go over all of the materials you have collected. Arrange your note cards according to your outline to identify any gaps in your research and to see if your ideas progress logically.

Match your notes to your thesis. Don't be surprised if you find holes and realize that you need to return to the library for more information before you begin to write.

Beginning Your First Draft

Depending upon the number of supporting details in your outline, writing a first draft may be a matter of simply "filling-in" your outline. Since the first draft is not meant for anyone but yourself, concentrate on getting just the main ideas down on paper. Allow your ideas to flow without too much concern for mechanical correctness or exact word choice. Your main goal is that you have a logical flow. You may think of a better way to organize your paper or present your ideas as you write—so stop and make any necessary changes as you work, revising your outline as necessary.

As you transfer your notes into your rough draft, you need to begin to expand on the material. Examine each point that you develop. Avoid using one note after another without offering your own thoughts and reactions. Your interpretation of the information will help the reader make sense of the material.

Remember, writing a first draft involves four steps:

Following the outline

Beginning each paragraph with a topic sentence that announces the point of the paragraph

Expanding each supporting point in the outline with your notes and evidence from your sources

Bridging all of the information together with your own thoughts, logic and transitions

Recall from the program the paragraph on the lottery. It began with the topic sentence:

> Advertising executives say there are two audiences they are particularly interested in, the working class person who might see the lottery as the chance of a lifetime and members of the upscale, yuppie market who have lots of cash to play the game.

The student was ready to insert her notes directly into her paper—and then remembered to check for the possibility of plagiarism.

Crediting Your Sources

As you transfer your notes into your first draft, be sure to *acknowledge the source for each note you use—whether it is a summary, paraphrase or direct quotation*. Failing to include this information will result in plagiarism. Plagiarism occurs in three ways:

1. Using someone's work word-for-word without citing the source and without using quotation marks
2. Using someone's work word-for-word and citing the source but omitting the quotation marks, thus giving the impression that it has been rewritten into your own words
3. Using someone's ideas without citing the source even though those ideas have been summarized or paraphrased into your own words

The student in the example checked her notes and decided to rephrase her paragraph:

> According to an article in *Gambling Times*, Les Perlman, an advertising executive with a leading agency in California, says there are two audiences agencies are particularly interested in, the working class....

By acknowledging her source the student was able to include specific information and avoid plagiarizing.

Using Connective Phrases

When transferring your notes into the rough draft, be sure your ideas connect logically. In some cases you will need only a few connective phrases, or transitions, to lead the reader from one idea to another. When the student writing about the lottery needed to get from one main idea (ad agencies) in her outline to another main idea (commercial ads and billboards), she needed a simple connective phrase which would allow the thought to flow logically.

> *In fact*, TV and newspaper ads and billboards are clearly aimed at these two audiences.

She then went on to provide examples,

> *For example....*

Connective phrases such as "In addition to," "In contrast," "For example," or "Ironically" can help bridge your ideas together. For a comprehensive list of connective phrases, see the Appendix on page 203.

Using Direct Quotations

Although direct quotations should be used sparingly, they do serve an important pur-pose. Use the following guidelines when considering including a direct quote.

Use Direct Quotes:

> To present an important, significant or key thought by an authority
>
> When the material is memorable or unique in its expression
>
> When the idea conflicts with the mainstream of thought
>
> When presenting specialized or technical information such as statistics

Creating Smooth Transitions

As explained, you can't just drop a quote or paraphrase into your paper and let it stand by itself. A quotation should be set up by a "lead-in," a sentence or two preceding it which helps introduce the idea. Recall this example of integrating a quote:

> New York City's school safety division has counted more than fifteen hundred incidents of violence in high schools in the past year. "It seems like almost once a week or every other week we have another kid get shot," says Safety Division Director Ed Muir. As a result of this....

Notice how the information in the first sentence sets the stage for the direct quote. Notice, too, that the direct quote adds color and a human dimension which would be lost if the idea were paraphrased. The last sentence develops the idea of the direct quote further and serves as a bridge to the next point.

Summaries, paraphrases, and direct quotes that are merely plugged into a paper are not effective; they serve only to call attention to themselves and interrupt the flow of ideas. As you write your first draft, try to integrate the thoughts from your note cards by using "lead-in" explanations and transitions.

Writing the Introduction and Conclusion

In the first draft of your paper, your introduction and conclusion will be sketchy. Because the final shape of your paper changes as you write, you may want to write the introduction and conclusion *after* writing the body paragraphs.

THE INTRODUCTION

Your introduction should accomplish the following:

1. Gain the attention and interest of your readers
2. Convince your readers that what you have to say is important and worthwhile
3. Explain the general context of your subject
4. Narrow the subject to your specific thesis which identifies your position

Recall from the program, two different introductions were written for the same thesis:

Thesis:

The increased number of kids killing kids in school is due primarily to the increased use and selling of crack cocaine.

The first introduction used a story:

Jim Johnson was on his way home to tell his mother he just made the high school football team when a classmate shot him in the back. James was the 100th youth to be murdered in this city this year. Many people think the rise in incidents of kids killing kids is due primarily to the increased use and selling of crack cocaine at the high school level....

The second introduction presented a statistic:

Since 1980, the crime rate among teenagers has tripled in this city. Murder has been the primary cause of youth deaths this year. The number of kids killing kids is on the increase. Many people think it's due to the increased use and selling of crack cocaine.

Either of these introductions could be used.

THE CONCLUSION

Like the introduction, the conclusion to your paper may be written after the body paragraphs have been fully developed. Your conclusion should summarize the main points of your paper and reinforce the position of your thesis. In the first draft stage, your conclusion will probably be sketchy. You may want to get your main ideas more sharply focused before you fine-tune your conclusion.

Before you put your first draft away and prepare to write your second draft, go through your paper once more to document your quotes and paraphrases with proper citations and a complete bibliography. You will then be ready to begin your second draft.

✔ Self Test

Mark each statement True or False.

1. _____ Transitions and explanations are needed to connect the thoughts from your note cards.

2. _____ Direct quotations add credibility and should be used as often as possible.

3. _____ Writing the first draft merely involves copying your notes to match the points in your outline.

4. _____ A quotation should be set up by one or two sentences which precede it to help introduce the idea.

5. _____ Rather than change the outline, you should try to make your material fit.

6. _____ If you have trouble getting started, you can begin your paper by developing the body paragraphs and write the introduction later.

7. _____ It is not necessary to credit a source for material that is *completely* rewritten in your own words.

8. _____ Supporting your thesis and convincing your readers are the two most important things to keep in mind as you write your paper.

9. _____ You should resist the temptation to change the order of presentation as you are writing.

Writing Assignments

1. The following assignment will give you practice in the vital task of *integrating* source material into the text of your paper. Write a paragraph in which you integrate each of the following direct quotations and paraphrases. Use the quotation or paraphrase *exactly* as it is written. Write one or two sentences setting up the source material and one or two sentences coming out of the material, perhaps leading to a related topic. An example is provided for you.

EXAMPLE:

Source material:

Noted writer and biologist, Thomas Riley, states, "Many species of birds require undisturbed watersheds of several acres or they will not reproduce" (12).

Source material integrated with sentences before and after:

Civilization's encroachment on wildlife habitats continues to put strains on the animal world. Birds are the latest species to feel the effects of "progress." **Noted writer and biologist, Thomas Riley, states, "Many species of birds require undisturbed watersheds of several acres or they will not reproduce" (12).** The type of natural environment Riley describes is being bulldozed over to make space for housing developments and shopping complexes. Decisions about land use must strike a balance between wildlife preservation and human progress because ultimately the two are interdependent.

EXERCISE:

    A. Source material:

        TV critic, Sarah Tobias, states, "Television game shows do not require contestants to go beyond superficial answers to questions. These shows reflect a world in which raw information is all that matters" (23).

    B. Source material:

        Study abroad programs provide students with the opportunity to gain valuable experience outside of the classroom (McCarroll 32).

    C. Source material:

        "The wholesale destruction of rain forests in South America and Indonesia will result in major disruptions in the planet's weather patterns in the next few decades," warns geologist Elizabeth Purvis (42).

  2. Leaf through a magazine of interest until you find an article with an introduction containing all four elements described in this lesson for introductions. In approximately 250 words, explain how the introduction accomplishes those four tasks.

Answer Key

1. T
2. F
3. F
4. T
5. F
6. T
7. F
8. T
9. F

Critiquing the First Draft

✔ Lesson Preview

In this lesson you will view a class in session as they evaluate their own essays and make necessary improvements. The instructor reminds the students of the importance of writing with exactness, explicitness, economy and elegance. You will see students formulate introductions which are clearly stated and draft conclusions that remain focused on the thesis. The two student essays critiqued in the program can be found at the end of the lesson.

Learning Objectives

After completing this lesson, you will be able to:

> ► Identify problems with citations and writing quality

> ► Revise and correct your own first draft by employing the principles reviewed including avoiding redundancy, focusing the thesis statement, strengthening concluding statements and avoiding mixed metaphors.

✔ View the Video Program

As you view the program, look for suggestions for improvement which you can use to improve your own first draft.

✔ Lesson Review

Critical Reading employs exactness, explicitness, economy, elegance

As you saw in the video, you can usually find ways to improve your writing. When you critique your first draft, check it for exactness, explicitness, economy of words and phrases, and elegance.

Exactness

When writing a paper on any topic, you should use words that express exactly what you mean to say. Your readers should not have to guess at your meaning. In the essay, "The Steroid Seduction," Frank used the term *clean* when he meant *drug-free*:

Of course, the ideal would be that all athletes would remain completely *clean*.

Frank assumed that his readers would understand the meaning of *clean* within the drug context. As the instructor pointed out, the implied opposite of clean is *dirty* and that isn't what Frank meant at all. His sentence was altered to read:

Of course, the ideal would be that all athletes would compete *drug-free*.

By using precise terms that clearly convey your thoughts, your readers will better understand the ideas in your essay. Recall the questions from Frank's introductory paragraph:

Should they take steroids or should they stay clean? Is their natural ability enough?

Frank then wrote:

These are common *thoughts* of a great many competitors.

Because he was expressing *questions*, not *thoughts*, Frank needed to revise his sentence:

These are common *questions* of a great many competitors.

The instructor cautioned the class to watch for sacrificing meaning by using words that are too general. Frank's statement about the athlete who used steroids for a pulled hamstring concluded with, "...he later was denied a gold metal in the 1987 World Championship due to the use of an illegal substance." The class argued that the term "illegal substance" was too general. "Illegal substance" could refer to heroin or any other drug. The instructor suggested that Frank find a more specific term.

Explicitness

When you omit key words, your meaning may be ambiguous. Recall the omission discussed in Mary's essay, "The Running Rage."

Much more blood than normal is pumped in and then pumped out. This increased volume stretches the heart and makes it more efficient.

Mary was not explicit when referring to "volume." She needed to explain *what* was stretching the heart. Her sentence was revised to read:

This increased *blood* volume stretches the heart and makes it more efficient.

To write explicitly, you must choose words that best describe what you are trying to express. In the following sentence, "offer" was changed to "opportunity"—a better choice.

Steroids ensure the athlete's speedy recovery; it presents a nearly irresistible *offer*.

As the instructor pointed out, steroids can't "offer" anything. It is more accurate to say that steroids presented *an opportunity* to the athlete. The sentence was revised to read:

Steroids ensure the athlete's speedy recovery; it presents a nearly irresistible *opportunity*.

In order to write explicit sentences, make sure you include all necessary words and use those words that express your ideas accurately.

Economy

To write economically you should try to use as few words as possible to say as much as possible. Whenever you can, use one word instead of two or three and avoid repeating phrases. Refer to the following sentence in Mary's essay:

Of all the exercises people are active in today, running is one of the healthiest ways to enjoy and help yourself.

It was decided that "are active in" could be replaced with an active verb. The sentence was revised to read:

Of all the exercises people *engage in* today, running is one of the healthiest...

In the following sentence from Frank's essay, the phrases "may be" and "seem to be" were discussed as redundant:

Often these injuries *may be* or *seem to be* insurmountable.

Using redundant terms can be compared to describing "a round circle." The instructor suggested selecting one phrase or the other.

Often these injuries *may be* insurmountable.

or

Often these injuries *seem to be* insurmountable.

Parallel form is another important aspect of writing an economical and focused paragraph. Recall the lack of uniformity in verbs in Mary's introduction:

Business men and women *don* their sneakers at lunch hour and *head* for the gym.

Students *are* occasionally *known to desert* the library with running shoes in hand.

Mothers *are seen jogging* behind strollers as well.

As the instructor pointed out, the sentences are not parallel because the verb forms are not consistent. By changing the verbs to active voice, present tense, Mary was able to write a clearer, more concise paragraph. The sentences were revised to read:

Students *desert* the library with running shoes in hand.

Mothers *jog* behind strollers as well.

Elegance

Check your essay to make sure your ideas are presented logically and that your sentences flow together smoothly. The following sentence from Mary's essay was identified as lacking clarity because it contains a dangling modifier.

As running begins, the lungs dilate.

This sentence needed to be rewritten because it is unclear what or who is running. Are the lungs running? The sentence was improved to read:

As one begins to run, his or her lungs dilate.

Using metaphors correctly will also enhance the style and elegance of an essay. Mixing metaphors will confuse your readers. Although Frank used garden imagery throughout his essay, he introduced a new and inconsistent image in his closing paragraph.

Steroids consistently bring controversy to the *center ring*....

As the instructor pointed out, "the center ring" is incongruent with the metaphor of the garden. The sentence needed to be reworked.

Introductions and Conclusions

When writing an introduction, you should begin with an attention grabber, introduce the general topic of the essay and narrow it to the thesis as quickly as possible. Returning again to Mary's essay, you may recall that Mary began by introducing her topic, fitness; she then focused on one aspect of fitness, running. Her introduction also included a plan of development—or imbedded outline—which provided information on what the body of the essay would cover. After stating that running is helpful, Mary then *mapped out* the following points to prove her statement:

It strengthens the heart, increases lung capacity and relieves tension.

The body paragraphs were then developed from the essay's thesis. Each of Mary's paragraphs corresponded to her imbedded outline.

Research papers as well as essays benefit from a plan of development or imbedded outline associated with the thesis statement.

In contrast, Frank's thesis sentence was unfocused and ambiguously stated:

Unfortunately, various reasons lead athletes to use strength-building drugs such as anabolic steroids to enhance their performance.

Frank was able to sharpen the focus and clarity of his thesis by rewording the sentence:

Unfortunately, today's athletes often use anabolic steroids to enhance their performance for a variety of reasons.

When writing a conclusion to your paper, you should simply summarize the main points and then gracefully exit the essay. Do not introduce new information; stay clearly focused on the content of your essay. As the instructor pointed out, Frank's conclusion is too lengthy. He was also guilty of introducing new ideas about athletes in general:

In a world where competition determines the greatness of both an individual and a nation, it is unfair to deny the incredible pressure that drives athletes of world-class standing.

Frank needed to revise the conclusion by shortening the paragraph and restating the main points.

Mary's essay began well, but then she introduced an inconsistent *term—yourself.*

Of all the exercises people are active in today, running is one of the healthiest ways to enjoy and help *yourself.*

Throughout her essay Mary had referred to the runner in the third person. When she used the term *yourself,* she switched to second person. This sentence was revised for consistency.

Running is one of the healthiest, most enjoyable ways to exercise.

Remember, in order to write a good conclusion, summarize your main points, stay focused on your topic, and exit your essay gracefully.

Writing Assignments

1. Select one of the two essays presented and rewrite it using some of the changes suggested in the program.

2. Using the reworked essay or another first draft, write the essay again applying some of the other techniques of good writing you have learned. Be prepared to defend your changes with principles of usage.

THE STEROID SEDUCTION

Every competing athlete entertains thoughts of becoming "the best." For some, it is a daydream; for others, it is a goal to be attained despite the cost. Has today's athlete been subtly seduced by the lure of greatness? Some argue that today's athlete is facing the proverbial serpent and the forbidden fruit scenario. Should they take steroids or should they stay clean? Is their natural ability enough? These are common thoughts of a great many competitors. Of course, the ideal would be that all athletes would compete clean. Unfortunately, various reasons lead athletes to use strength-building drugs such as anabolic steroids to enhance their performance.

Recurring injuries plague numerous athletes. Often these injuries may be or seem to be insurmountable. Studies reveal that anabolic steroids accelerate the healing process of muscle tissue. Steroids ensure the athlete speedy recovery; it presents a nearly irresistible offer. Ben Johnson is an unfortunate example of an athlete who opted to use steroids for healing purposes. Although the drug served to rectify the ailment of a pulled hamstring, he later was denied a gold medal in the 1987 World Championship due to the use of an illegal substance.

Steroids provide enormous amounts of energy, causing the athlete to easily overcome any fatigue he or she may be experiencing. Even though steroids negatively affect the brain and reproductive systems, they rebuild muscle tissue. This allows the athlete to engage in more frequent and rigorous workouts. Steroids alleviate any muscle soreness that results from intensive training. Reproducing muscle cells give increased energy levels, resulting in more strength.

An athlete cannot live on dreams forever. In many cases, after years of rigorous training and self denial, athletes are forced to recognize their limitations. Despite the intensity of their hard work, they feel inadequate, frustrated and cheated. It is often at this time in their career that they are able to rationalize the use of steroids. It is the opportunity to raise their level of performance from good to best. Suddenly the gymnasium takes on garden-like qualities.

Steroids consistently bring controversy to the center ring, whether used for healing injuries, gaining energy or improving athletic performance. In a world where competition determines the greatness of both an individual and a nation, it is unfair to deny the incredible pressure that drives athletes of world-class standing. In the minds of many great athletes, being second best is not being a good American. Before banishing the athlete who would opt for legalization of steroids or use steroids despite their illegal status, consider the manipulation that occurs in the daily bombardment of advertisement schemes. You can almost picture the serpent raising its ugly head and hear the coaxing, luring, melodic promise--you can have it all, and you can be the best. The American public is part of a seduction every day. You almost can't blame the athlete who sides with Eve--or can you?

Submitted by Frank Carson

THE RUNNING RAGE

Fitness is a buzz word of the ninety's. People of all shapes and sizes are integrating exercise into their hectic, on-the-go life styles. Business men and women don their sneakers at lunch hour and head for the gym or the park. Students are occasionally known to desert the library with running shoes in hand. Mothers are seen jogging behind strollers as well. Staying fit has become everyone's job. Of all the exercises to choose from, running is probably the most convenient and beneficial. Running is helpful because it strengthens the heart, increases lung capacity and relieves tension.

Engaging in an endurance exercise such as running, guarantees the strengthening of the heart muscle. Much more blood than normal is pumped in and then pumped out. This increased volume stretches the heart and makes it more efficient. By running regularly, the volume of blood is maintained at a higher level thus supplying the heart with a greater oxygen content.

Another benefit resulting from a running routine is increased lung capacity. As running begins, the lungs dilate expanding the area through which oxygen passes. By stretching the lungs, they are capable of handling a larger air supply more efficiently. This expanded oxygen supply is then transported to all parts of the body.

Running not only strengthens the body but promises a healthy mind and spirit. A good run is a great stress reliever and can take care of a headache as well as any aspirin. Physical exhilaration often results in mental stimulation. During a run one is able to reflect on the day's events and gain new perspective on any given situation or problem. The runner completes the exercise with renewed energy, ready to face the challenges at hand.

Of all the exercises people are active in today, running is one of the healthiest ways to enjoy and help yourself. Runners are all ages and it costs very little to get started. Running has revolutionized America's approach to exercise and a healthy life style. Whether on lunch hour, after work or school, running has become part of the daily routine of the entire family. There's no stopping now.

Submitted by Mary Sullivan

L E S S O N   12

Crediting Your Sources

✔ Lesson Preview

Just like a credit roll at the end of a movie, a Works Cited list at the end of a paper gives proper credit to the ideas and research included in your paper. The Works Cited list lets your readers see the extent of your research—how current it is and what types of sources were consulted—and it helps your readers place your writing within a wider context. Readers familiar with your subject can recognize sources they have encountered before; readers unfamiliar with the topic are given information they can use to locate the source materials themselves.

Although there are several forms or styles for documentation, most colleges require documenting according to either the MLA (Modern Language Association) or the APA (American Psychological Association) style. Because MLA is preferred in most English classes, this lesson will present the MLA format in more detail. Check with your instructor to find out which documentation style is required for your class. Whichever format you use, you must follow it *very carefully.*

In this lesson you will learn how to cite each type of source (book, magazine, film, audio cassette, etc.) within the text of your paper. You will also learn how to document your source material for special circumstances such as using sources without authors, using more than one source by the same author, and including direct quotations. Finally, you will learn how to prepare a Works Cited or Reference list in the appropriate format.

Learning Objectives

After completing this lesson, you will be able to:

➤ Prepare a Works Cited list using MLA format or a Reference list using APA format

➤ Follow the required format for in-text MLA or APA documentation

➤ Avoid plagiarism

Use the appropriate format to document for:

➤ Sources without authors

• More than one source by the same author

• Direct quotes of more than four lines

✔ View the Video Program

As you view the program, look for varied and interesting (but technically correct) ways of citing references within the text of the research paper.

✔ Lesson Review

As you have seen, a Works Cited or Reference list gives credit to all the books, articles, films, tapes, records, interviews and all other sources used in putting your paper together. Crediting your sources is important for several reasons:

It gives the reader insight into the *extent* of your research

It provides readers information for *locating* the source material themselves

It allows you to *recognize* the ideas and research of others who contributed to your ideas

By acknowledging the information in the paper that is not your own, you can avoid plagiarism. Plagiarism, as you know, is the use of other people's words and ideas as if they were your own. By crediting the original writer, you are not implying that those ideas are strictly your own.

> **If a statement or idea isn't your own, you should document it.**

Document a source within your paper when:

1. An idea belonging to someone else is expressed in your own words (paraphrased or summarized)
2. A direct quotation is used (sparingly)
3. Any fact or statistic is used that is not widely known or accepted

Documenting Your Sources

The main reason for using a documentation system is to provide enough information about the source within your paper to direct the reader to the corresponding entry in your Works Cited or Reference list at the end of your paper. Traditionally, the term bibliography was used for books and articles used in writing a paper. But today, with a greater variety of source materials, the term bibliography has been replaced by "Works Cited" or "References" to encompass the broader meaning.

While there are several forms or styles for documentation, the two styles used predominantly in colleges, MLA and APA, were presented in the program. Because the MLA style (endorsed by the Modern Language Association) is preferred in most English classes, the MLA style was explained in greater detail.

Using the MLA Style

Creating a Works Cited List

The Works Cited list provides a complete and detailed accounting of all sources used in your paper. It is the only place for readers to obtain detailed information about your sources. In the Works Cited list a reader can obtain specific information which includes the name of the author, the complete title of the work, the date of publication, the place of publication, and the publisher. Of course specific details will change according to the type of reference used.

When listing publication information, give the city of publication, the publisher's name, and the year of publication. Note that hanging indentation is used, i.e., the first line is flush with the left margin and all subsequent lines for that entry are indented five spaces. Entries are alphabetized by the author's last name (when there is one); all articles *(a, an, the)* are ignored. When listing the titles of books, capitalize the major words in the title and underline the entire title.

A SAMPLE WORKS CITED PAGE FOLLOWING MLA GUIDELINES:

WORKS CITED

Bartram, David. <u>Quark Hunters</u>. New York: Macmillan, 1990.

"Faulkner, William." Encyclopaedia Britannica. 1985 ed.

Finch, Charles Edward. "The Life Extension Revolution." <u>Vitality and Aging</u>. Ed. Alfred Holter. Garden City: Anchor, 1990.

Johnson, Lawrence, ed. <u>Population Explosion</u>. New York: Bowker, 1990.

Kasdan, Lawrence, dir. <u>The Big Chill</u>. With William Hurt, Kevin Kline, Glenn Close, and Meg Tilly. Columbia, 1984.

Lexander, John. "A Study in Longevity." <u>Journal of American Geriatrics Society</u> 40 (1988): 367-72.

Schroeder, James, Walter C. Harding, and Michael Meyer. <u>Handbook of Political Science</u>. San Diego: Harcourt, 1987.

Simon, Paul. "Under African Skies." <u>Graceland</u>. Warner Bros., 7599-25447-4, 1986.

United States. Dept. of Housing and Urban Development. <u>Wise Home Buying</u>. Washington: GPO, 1986.

Walford, Robert Louis. "How People Will Live To Be 100 or More." <u>U.S. News and World Report</u> 17 July 1989: 58-60.

---. <u>Maximum Life Span</u>. New York: Stein, 1988.

"We've Never Asked a Woman Before." <u>Time</u> 13 Mar. 1990: 44.

Format for a Book

In the video program, the following entry was used to illustrate a book with one author:

Toffler, Alvin. <u>Future Shock</u>. New York: Random, 1970.

Note that "Random" refers to the publishing company, "Random House." With the more recent MLA format, the publisher's name is shortened appropriately while remaining identifiable enabling the reader to locate the source. Also note that the name of the *city* in which the book was published can be listed without the state if the city is fairly well known as New York, Los Angeles or London. Lesser known cities need to be followed by the state.

Format for Magazine and Newspaper Articles

When formatting an article, list the author's full name (last name first), the title of the article (in quotation marks), the title of the magazine or journal (underlined), the date of publication (day precedes month and year) and the page number. The following example was used to illustrate a magazine article in the video program:

"Beyond the White House." <u>Time</u> 14 May 1988: 94.

Note: When no author is identified, the title of the article becomes the first entry.

A Works Cited page needs to be constructed with diligent attention to detail, so it is necessary to have a grammar handbook or other style book at hand to consult for each entry.

Format for Electronic Resources

ACADEMIC ABSTRACTS ON CD-ROM
Author's Last Name, First Name. Rev. of <u>Book Title</u> by Book's Author. <u>Magill Book Reviews</u>. Academic Abstracts, Month Year, item number.

GROLIER'S ELECTRONIC ENCYCLOPEDIA
Author's Last Name, First Name. "Article Title." <u>Grolier's Electronic Encyclopaedia.</u> Date.

NEWSBANK MICROFICHE
Author's Last Name, First Name. "Article Title," <u>Newspaper Name</u> Day Month Year. Newsbank, Section Name, year, fiche number, grid number.

SIRS
Author's Last Name, First Name. "Title of the Article." <u>Journal Title.</u> Date: pages. SIRS Researcher CD-ROM.

For electronic media, such as online information, online abstracts, online journals-subscriber based, online journals-general access (e-mail), electronic data files, electronic databases, computer programs, computer software, and programming languages, consult the *Handbook for Writers of Research Papers*.

Citing Within the Text

In addition to the Works Cited list at the end of your paper, you need to document your sources *within* the paper. Whenever you use information from an outside source, whether it's a direct quotation or a paraphrase, you need to provide enough information about the source to direct your readers to the corresponding entry on your Works Cited page. With the MLA format, only two pieces of information are required: the author's last name and a page number. As you saw in the video, the following citation at the end of the quotation was adequate to refer the reader to its complete entry in the Works Cited list:

"Once all of the available life boats had been dispatched from the sinking <u>Titanic,</u> those doomed to remain on and go down with the ship experienced an uncanny sense of calm" (Lord 109).

The reader was referred to this entry:

Lord, Walter. <u>A Night to Remember</u>. New York: Holt, 1976.

The author and page number will provide enough information for the reader to locate the entry unless there are two authors with the same last name or if one author has more than one entry. In either of these cases, more information must be given.

When you use more than one work by the same author, give the author's name, a shortened title and the page number. In the video you saw that the student used another book by Walter Lord, *The Night Lives On*. The citation (Lord 127) does not indicate to which book the student was referring. By including part of the title in the entry (Lord, <u>A Night to</u> 201), the correct book was referenced.

When two different authors have the same last name, list the author's full name in the text. In the program a student used Susan Cheever's book, *Home Before Dark*, as well as John Cheever's book, *The Wapshot Chronicle*. The correct reference became clear only when the author's full name was included (Susan Cheever 101).

When no author is designated, the source is referenced by the first word in the title of the article. In the program ("Bone" 54) was the correct citation for an article with no author. The full entry on the Works Cited page was listed as:

"Bone Booster." <u>Time</u> 23 Jan. 1989: 54.

When an author's name is included within a sentence, you need to include only the page number in parenthesis after the sentence for referencing. Recall the example from the lesson:

According to Lord, the <u>Titanic</u> was the last ocean liner to ever sail with too few lifeboats (127).

Since it was clear that Lord was the author of the book, it was not necessary to repeat the information. Authors' names are often included as part of the text as a "lead-in" to the sentence.

When a quotation is longer than four lines, set it apart from the rest of the text with *block formatting*. Indent ten spaces from the left and right margins, but do not use quotation marks. The citation appears at the end of the quoted passage, but the end punctuation precedes the parenthetical documentation. Consider the following example:

> William Metz and Allen Hammond, authors of <u>Solar Energy in America,</u> discuss the benefits of solar energy:

> > It falls on everyone and can be put to use by individuals and small groups of people. The public enthusiasm for solar energy is perhaps as much a reflection of its unusual accessibility as it is a vote for the environmental kindliness and inherent renewability of energy from the sun. The number of solar-heated houses built in the United States has doubled approximately every 8 months since 1973. (18)

Using the APA Style

APA, the style endorsed by the American Psychological Association, is often required for classes in the social sciences. You may be asked to write papers following APA guidelines for history, psychology, sociology and education classes. Remember to check with your instructors to see which format they prefer before you begin writing.

Creating a Reference List

When listing sources at the end of your paper, APA style requires a list of References (as opposed to Works Cited for MLA). Like the Works Cited list, the list of References is all-inclusive and should include detailed information on each source used in writing your paper—whether a book, magazine article, government document, movie, recording or personal interview. Do not, however, reference those sources which you may have read but are not cited within the text of your paper.

Like the MLA format, hanging indentation (first line flush left with margin) is used. Note, however, that subsequent lines are indented *three* spaces, not five as in MLA. Entries are alphabetized by author when there is one. Unlike MLA, however, note that only the first word in the title of a book or article is capitalized; all subsequent words in the title are in lower case. The entire title is underlined. Following APA format, note that the date of publication follows the author's name. The following example was used in the video program:

> Wilson, K. (1985). <u>Rural telephone sagas</u>. New York: Dell.

Note also that the name of the *city* in which the book was published can be listed *without the state* if the city is fairly well known such as New York, Los Angeles, or London. Lesser known cities need to be followed by the state. As with any task involving documentation, a reference list must be constructed with painstaking accuracy.

Format for Electronic Resources

Although a brief list of examples of some common sources of electronic data follows, for electronic media, such as online information, online abstracts, online journals-subscriber based, online journal-general access (e-mail), electronic data files, electronic databases, computer programs, computer software, and programming languages, consult the *Publication Manual of the American Psychological Association.*

ACADEMIC ABSTRACTS on CD-ROM
Author's Last Name, First Initial. (date). Rev. of <u>Book Title</u> by Book's Author. [CD-ROM]. <u>Magill Book Reviews</u>. Full-text from: Ebsco CD: Academic Abstracts Full-Text Elite Item: item number.

GROLIER'S ELECTRONIC ENCYCLOPEDIA
Author's Last Name, First Initial. (date). Article Title [CD-ROM]. In <u>Grolier's Electronic Encyclopedia</u>. Danbury, CT: Grolier, Inc.

NEWSBANK MICROFICHE
Author's Last Name, First Initial. (year, month day). Title of the article [microfiche]. <u>Newspaper Name</u>, pp. Full-test from: Newsbank Electronic Information Systems: Newsbank, Section Name: year, fiche number, grid number.

SIRS
Author's Last Name, First Initial. Middle Initial. (year, Month). Article title. <u>Journal Name</u>, pp. From <Volume year> [SIRS Researcher CD-ROM year].

A SAMPLE REFERENCE LIST FOLLOWING APA GUIDELINES:

REFERENCES

Bartram, D. (1990). <u>Quark hunters</u>. New York: Macmillan.

Department of Housing and Urban Development. (1986). <u>Wise home buying</u> S/N 023-000-00752-5) Washington, DC: U.S. Government Printing Office.

Faulkner, William. (1985). <u>Encyclopaedia Britannica</u> (Vol. 4, p. 249). Chicago: Encyclopaedia Britannica.

Finch, C. E. (1990). The life extension revolution. In A. Holter (Ed.), <u>Vitality and aging</u> (pp. 112-141). Garden City, NY: Anchor.

Johnson, L. (Ed.). (1990). <u>Population explosion</u>. New York: Bowker.

Kasdan, L. (Director). (1984). <u>The big chill</u> [Film]. Hollywood, CA: Columbia.

Lexander, J. (1988). A study in longevity. <u>Journal of American Geriatrics Society</u>, 40, 367-372.

Schroeder, J., Harding, W. C., & Meyer, M. (1987). <u>Handbook of political science</u>. San Diego: Harcourt.

Simon, P. (Performing Artist). (1986). Under African skies. <u>Graceland</u> (Cassette Recording No. 7599-25447-4). Los Angeles: Warner Bros.

Walford, R. L. (1988). <u>Maximum life span</u>. New York: Stein.

Walford, R. L. (1989, July 17). How people will live to be 100 or more. <u>U.S. News and World Report</u>, pp. 58-60.

We've never asked a woman before. (1990, March 13). <u>Time</u>, p. 44.

Citing Within the Text

When citing an author's work *within* the text of your paper, briefly identify the source so that your readers can locate the information in your alphabetical reference list. Include the author's last name and the year of publication (Lord, 1976).

When citing the source of a direct quotation, give the author, year, and page number in parentheses in the text. Note the abbreviation for page (p.) or pages (pp.) is also included:

(Lord, 1976, p. 109).

Compare this to the following MLA format for within-text references:

(Lord 109).

Note that with APA format, the publication date is included and designates the work, thereby eliminating the need for a title when you have more than one work by an author. When citing an author's name within a sentence, the publication date immediately follows the name; the page number is then placed at the end of the passage. For example:

According to Lord (1976), the Titanic was the last ocean liner ever to sail with too few lifeboats (p. 127).

Although the MLA and APA styles are widely used in colleges and universities, many other formats are available and may be required for certain disciplines. Style manuals for many disciplines can be found in your college library. As you progress in your college work, you should become familiar with the documentation style preferred in your major field of study. If unsure, check with your instructor to see which style is preferred.

✔ Self Test

Using either the MLA or APA format, punctuate and capitalize each of the following direct quotations. Check your answers with the answer sheets that follow. If you use APA format, it will be necessary to insert the publication date and the abbreviation for page numbers.

EXAMPLE (MLA format):

"The growth rate of South Korea was cut nearly in half last year," states Russell Watson, "and the inflation rate has reached double digits with no sign of slowing down" (38).

EXAMPLE (APA format):

"The growth rate of South Korea was cut nearly in half last year," states Russell Watson (1990), "and the inflation rate has reached double digits with no sign of slowing down" (p. 38).

EXERCISE:

1. Now for the first time in his political life notes political writer Mark Hertsgaard George Bush is suddenly called upon not to relay orders but to give them

   Page 84; publication date, 1990.

2. In a recent <u>Newsweek</u> article, Dennis Williams offers ideas for improving our public schools

   one way to improve the quality of teachers is to attract college students who are majoring in academic subjects. Kentucky leads the way with "forgiveness loans": students majoring in needed academic fields who agree to take minimum certification courses and teach for three years in the state's public schools need not pay back the money

   Page 56; publication date, 1991.

3. From the outset, Flannery O'Connor had the instinct of every good writer notes critic Sally Fitzgerald she created Southern figures especially in short stories like Greenleaf whom her imagination could bring to concrete life

   Page 20; publication date, 1984.

4. What were we endorsing when we wished Mickey Mouse a happy birthday Mamet asks

   Page 110; publication date, 1981

5. In the 80s, drama took on a more serious and socially concerned tone, highlighting characters who were searching for values, identity and self-fulfillment (Delgado)

   Quoted Phrase: searching for values, identity and self-fulfillment
   Page 10; publication date, 1989

6. A controversial Billings Gazette editorial contends owls have the right to the same consideration as loggers ("Owls or Employed Loggers")

    Page 11B; publication date, 1990

7. Philosopher David Glidden writes during the sixth century B.C. the elements of a successful life were considered beyond a person's control, thus prompting Greek sage Solon to say call no man happy until that man is dead

    Page 114; publication date, 1986

8. Arts at the most basic level provide entertainment for humans but they also offer a voice of hope which humans should not ignore (Clancy)

    Quoted Phrase: a voice of hope
    Page 17; publication date, 1986

9. Jim Schnell states, English has become the predominant language in the international community

    Page 118; publication date, 1989

Writing Assignments

Determine whether the student version following each original excerpt is an example of correct scholarship or whether it is an example of plagiarism. If it is plagiarism, give the reason.

1. **ORIGINAL**

    American Presidents are not mere victims, buffeted by the circumstances of their histories and experiences; they are active agents in the midst of life, coping and resilient. I see them not as segmented characters but as whole men, capable of growth. (page 33)

    Lerner, Max. "Of Presidents and Their Splendours & Miseries." Encounter 65.1 (1985): 33-39.

    STUDENT VERSION

    In order to understand American Presidents, one must see them as active agents in the midst of life and not as segmented characters buffeted by circumstance (Lerner 33).

2. **ORIGINAL**

    Back in 1954 Mercedes took a hugely successful racing car, the 300SL, and with minor changes turned it into a sports car for sale to the public. It caused a sensation. For one thing, it looked like no other car on the road. The doors were hinged at the top, so that when they were open it resembled a bird in flight. (page 56)

    Berendt, John. "The Mercedes 500SL." Esquire May 1990: 56-57.

STUDENT VERSION

<u>Esquire</u> magazine notes that Mercedes redesigned its 1954 300SL racing machine into a sensational road car that had doors hinged at the top rather than the sides.

3. **ORIGINAL**

Opening a franchise from scratch isn't the only option for those interested in going into business for themselves. Often existing franchises are on sale and currently resales are responsible for nearly 50% of the activity of business brokerage services. Changing hands most are franchises in fast food, auto markets, quick printing and video rental shops. The average ownership of a franchise is 4.8 years. (page 12A)

Steinberg, Carol. "Resales Offer Ready-Made Opportunities." <u>USA Today</u> 7 Sept. 1989: 8A+.

STUDENT VERSION

Carol Steinberg reports that franchises change hands on average every five years. Changing hands most are franchises in fast food, auto markets, quick printing and video rental shops, says Steinberg (12A).

4. **ORIGINAL**

During the 1950's anti-Communism implied more than opposition to a particular regime or even a political philosophy. It suggested a comprehensive counter-ideology of its own, a system of total politics, one consumed by what it opposes and which therefore constructs a political universe in terms that derive almost exclusively from the felt imperatives of the conflict with the enemy. (page 35)

Nuechterlein, James. "William F. Buckley, Jr. and American Conservatism." <u>Commentary</u> 85.6 (1988): 31-44.

STUDENT VERSION

Anti-Communism of the 1950's was "a comprehensive counter-ideology of its own" that developed as a result of "the felt imperatives of the conflict with the enemy" (Nuechterlein 32).

5. **ORIGINAL**

For Southern Baptists the relevant doctrines are the primacy of the individual conscience, the autonomy of the local church, and the concept of the preaching ministry as a direct calling from God. The ability of women to respond to the call to the ministry and the power of local churches to ordain them are squarely within the Baptist tradition. (page 123)

Rosenberg, Ellen M. "Serving Jesus in the South: Southern Baptist Women under Assault from the New Right." <u>Women in the South</u>. Ed. Holly F. Matthews. Athens: U of Georgia (1989): 122-32.

STUDENT VERSION

According to Ellen Rosenberg, Southern Baptist women are allowed to join the ministry. The fact that local churches can ordain them places the church squarely within the Baptist tradition (123).

Answer Key—Self Test

1. MLA:

"Now, for the first time in his political life," notes political writer Mark Hertsgaard, "George Bush is suddenly called upon not to relay orders but to give them" (84).

APA:

"Now, for the first time in his political life," notes political writer Mark Hertsgaard (1990), "George Bush is suddenly called upon not to relay orders but to give them" (p. 84).

2. MLA:

In a recent <u>Newsweek</u> article, Dennis Williams offers ideas for improving our public schools:

One way to improve the quality of teachers is to attract college students who are majoring in academic subjects. Kentucky leads the way with "forgiveness loans": students majoring in needed academic fields who agree to take minimum certification courses and teach for three years in the state's public schools need not pay back the money. (56)

APA:

In a recent <u>Newsweek</u> article, Dennis Williams (1991) offers ideas for improving our public schools:

One way to improve the quality of teachers is to attract college students who are majoring in academic subjects. Kentucky leads the way with "forgiveness loans:" students majoring in needed academic fields who agree to take minimum certification courses and teach for three years in the state's public schools need not pay back the money. (p. 56)

3. MLA:

"From the outset, Flannery O'Connor had the instinct of every good writer," notes critic Sally Fitzgerald. "She created Southern figures, especially in short stories like 'Greenleaf,' whom her imagination could bring to concrete life" (20).

APA:

"From the outset, Flannery O'Connor had the instinct of every good writer," notes critic Sally Fitzgerald (1984). "She created Southern figures, especially in short stories like 'Greenleaf,' whom her imagination could bring to concrete life" (p. 20).

4. MLA:
    "What were we endorsing when we wished Mickey Mouse a happy birthday?"
    Mamet asks (110).

    APA:
    "What were we endorsing when we wished Mickey Mouse a happy birthday?"
    Mamet (1981) asks (p. 110).

5. MLA:
    In the 80's, drama took on a more serious and socially concerned tone, high-
    lighting characters who were "searching for values, identity and self-fulfill-
    ment" (Delgado 10).

    APA:
    In the 80's, drama took on a more serious and socially concerned tone, high-
    lighting characters who were "searching for values, identity and self-fulfill-
    ment" (Delgado, 1989, p. 10).

6. MLA:
    A controversial <u>Billings Gazette</u> editorial contends, "Owls have the right to the
    same consideration as loggers" ("Owls or" 11B).

    APA:
    A controversial <u>Billings Gazette</u> editorial contends, "Owls have the right to the
    same consideration as loggers" ("Owls or," 1990, p. 11B).

7. MLA:
    Philosopher David Glidden writes, "During the sixth century B.C. the elements
    of a successful life were considered beyond a person's control, thus prompting
    Greek sage Solon to say, 'Call no man happy until that man is dead'" (114).

    APA:
    Philosopher David Glidden (1986) writes, "During the sixth century B.C. the
    elements of a successful life were considered beyond a person's control, thus
    prompting Greek sage Solon to say, 'Call no man happy until that man is
    dead'" (p. 114).

8. MLA:
    Arts, at the most basic level, provide entertainment for humans, but they also
    offer "a voice of hope" which humans should not ignore (Clancy 17).

    APA:
    Arts, at the most basic level, provide entertainment for humans, but they also
    offer "a voice of hope" which humans should not ignore (Clancy, 1986, p. 17).

9. MLA:
    Jim Schnell states, "English has become the predominant language in the
    international community" (118).

    APA:
    Jim Schnell (1989) states, "English has become the predominant language in
    the international community" (p. 118).

Answer Key—Writing Assignments

1. **PLAGIARIZED**

   Although the order of the wording has been changed and the source is correctly identified, word-for-word phrases have been used without quotation marks.

2. **PLAGIARIZED**

   The documentation is incomplete in the student version; author and page number are not included.

3. **PLAGIARIZED**

   The documentation is correct but exact wording has been used in the student version without quotation marks.

4. **CORRECT**

   Correctly documented with quotation marks around phrases used verbatim.

5. **PLAGIARIZED**

   The documentation is correct but the last phrase is taken verbatim without quotation marks.

L E S S O N 13

Preparing the Second Draft

Revising, Revising, Revising

✔ Lesson Preview

If you have ever worked on an art project, a home improvement plan, or taken on any major project for that matter, you know that when you come back to it after a period of time, you always notice ways to improve it. Leaving the project for awhile allows you to return with a fresh perspective—to look at it more objectively. The same is true for writing. Even though you may like your work at first, if you give your ideas time to incubate, you can probably find ways of improving your writing. This "re-seeing" process is known as revision; it helps you focus on your paper's ideas and content. In this lesson you will learn to look more critically at your paper and make improvements.

Although your main concern in revision is whether your body paragraphs develop logically and relate to the thesis, you must also look at the introduction and conclusion for possible revision. Since the introduction lures your readers into your paper and the conclusion leaves them with a final impression, these sections of your paper are very important. In this lesson you will learn a number of ways to open and close your essay as well as some common pitfalls you should try to avoid.

Learning Objectives

After completing this lesson you will be able to:

▶ Critically review the organization and idea development in your paper

▶ Check your paper for possible revisions using the following strategies:

  • Checking for relevance and looking for unnecessary details

  • Looking for holes or places that need further explanation

  • Eliminating bias while preserving argumentative slant

  • Improving description

  • Polishing and reworking your introduction and conclusion

  • Identifying and correcting any logical fallacies

▶ Develop an introduction to your paper using one of the following techniques:

  • Starting with an anecdote

  • Presenting startling facts or statistics

- Employing sharp contrast
- Presenting historical information

➤ Formulate a conclusion using one of the following techniques:
- Restating your thesis
- Tying in an anecdote from the introduction
- Suggesting a course of action
- Ending with a prediction

✔ View the Video Program

As you view the program, look for examples of writing containing unnecessary details, as well as writing containing holes which need further explanations. Be prepared to explain the difference between writing with slant versus writing with bias.

✔ Lesson Review

Revising Body Paragraphs

As you have seen, your main concern in revision is whether your body paragraphs develop logically and relate to the thesis. Each paragraph in your paper should advance one main idea through your topic sentence; all other sentences in that paragraph should elaborate on that idea. Paragraphs should be organized in a logical order that your readers can follow. A checklist of revision considerations may help ensure your paper's coherence.

Revision Considerations

Ask yourself the following:

Are there any unnecessary details in my paper?

Are there any places where I should add more examples, explanations or facts?

Have I used a reasonable slant?

Have I prevented bias from creeping into my paper?

Have I included enough description?

Are my facts accurate and noncontradictory?

Checking for Unnecessary Details

Sometimes when writing, you may generate very interesting ideas that do not relate to your thesis. Recall the example in the program in which one student included information from medical research to support her thesis—teenagers are responsible for spreading AIDS. In a supporting sentence she offered a possible explanation:

One reason for this is that adolescents often do not feel their own mortality and therefore take greater chances.

The student then wrote about drugs and reckless driving:

> Many students in last year's graduating class were known to flirt with death on several occasions. Some experimented with different combinations of drugs and drove recklessly. Last year more high school seniors died in car wrecks than any other graduating class had in previous years.

This student was off on a tangent; she provided an unrelated example—instead of writing about teenagers and risk taking, the student strayed to the topic of drugs. This made it difficult to move on to the next thought.

To keep on track, ask yourself questions about your topic. In the previous example, the student could have asked: "Why would teenagers spread AIDS?" "In what ways would they spread the disease?" "To what extent?" If she had asked herself these questions, she would have remained focused on her topic and written a more coherent paper.

Filling in Holes

Look for holes in your writing—places where you have not included enough information. When you raise specific points in your paper, you must elaborate on those points to help prove your argument. When you omit essential information, your ideas will be lacking in development. Consider the following example from the program:

> Airline executives say they have statistics to prove air travel is safer today than it was ten years ago. Despite this, there have been five major accidents in the past two years.

In this example the student failed to cite the statistics needed to explain the significance of the second sentence. Were there more airline crash victims ten years ago? Is air travel safer today? How do you know? Notice how the revised version provides the missing information and aids in the overall understanding:

> Airline executives say air travel is safer today than it was ten years ago. They base this claim on a study which indicates that plane crashes occurred on an average of three a year in the early '80s, whereas only one occurs each year on the average today. Regardless of these claims, air travel has not necessarily improved. There have been five major accidents in the past two years.

Checking for Slant vs. Bias

Another important consideration when revising is determining whether you are writing with a slant or whether you have taken a position in your paper which includes bias. **Slant** provides your reader with a point of view; it adds interest and flair to your writing. Recall the ballooning example. Several different points of view of the same event were provided. Writing with a slant helps make your writing more lively and imaginative as opposed to being bland and mechanical. Recall the following sentence written with slant:

> He blew up, like a sudden rainstorm that came without warning, then as suddenly he smiled. as if the clouds had parted.

Notice that the student carefully chose adjectives, adverbs, and action verbs which add zest and interest to the sentence.

Bias, on the other hand, is a prejudice which ignores facts or contradictory evidence; a bias is a judgment based on emotion. Bias does not belong in academic writing, whereas writing with a slant or a point of view does. As you saw in the video example, the student was guilty of writing with bias when she wrote:

> He was a disgusting man with an unpredictable temper and he had no right to have children.

This is an *opinion*; it can't be proved or disproved. In an effort to avoid bias, some writers revert to dry, non-descriptive writing. Recall the images in the following sentence:

> Music known as "heavy metal" is often performed by people who wear face make-up, dress in costumes and shout rather than sing.

From this description the reader could have easily imagined a clown at a children's birthday party! Remember that your job as a writer is to help your reader imagine what you see. In the revised sentence, the descriptions are more accurate and detailed:

> Performances of heavy metal music often contain demonic overtones—from the satanic black costumes and black fingernails of the musicians, to larger-than-life backdrops which pulsate...

Again, note the choice of adjectives, adverbs and verbs which help create rich descriptions and add zest to the prose.

Verifying Accuracy

Another aspect of revising your draft is checking the accuracy of your facts. Make sure you haven't included contradictory information. If you do find contradictions, go back to your sources. The student in the program wrote about an artist who relied upon his imagination to paint; he later wrote about the same artist's use of live models. After checking his sources and finding that both of these statements were true, he revised his sentence:

> Although Degas primarily painted from imagination, he occasionally relied on real models.

If you can't attribute the contradictory information to expert opinion, you can simply acknowledge that the problem exists.

Polishing the Introduction and Conclusion

When preparing the second draft of your paper, you should also work on polishing your introduction and conclusion. Since the introduction lures the reader into a paper and the conclusion leaves the final impression, these two sections are very important.

First check to be sure that the introduction containing your thesis relates to the body of the paper. The same is true for the conclusion—does it relate to the thesis? If so, you are ready to rework these sections into something more than mere statements of intent or summary.

106

The Introduction

The purpose of an introduction is to bait your readers so they will want to read the entire piece. An introduction should be interesting and appealing. There are a number of ways to introduce a paper. Some of the more common techniques are:

Start with an anecdote

Present some startling facts or statistics

Use sharp contrast

Present some historical background on the subject

Starting with a story or an *anecdote* requires a specific example that supports your thesis. For example, you may want to begin with a story about a self-sufficient ninety-year-old woman to lead into a thesis which states elderly people are better off remaining in their homes.

Another way to introduce your thesis is to open with *startling facts or statistics*. For instance, the following statements should grab most readers' attention:

Half the red spruce trees in the Northeast above 2,500 feet, which flourished in the early 1960's, are dead today.

or

The U.S. Department of Education last week reported that nearly twenty-one million adults in the U.S. cannot read. Nearly one in five Americans cannot read well enough to perform the simplest tasks such as writing checks or addressing envelopes.

Opening your essay with *sharp contrasts* is another effective method of introduction. For example:

Despite their obsession with dieting, Americans seem to grow fatter every year.

or

Most people think of Peace Corps volunteers as idealistic young people in khaki shorts digging wells in Tanzania. That image will need some revision when volunteers start arriving in the world's newest developing area—Eastern Europe.

Finally, you may use *historical background* to introduce your thesis. To open a paper with the thesis that war in the Middle East has forced people to re-evaluate war, the writer could provide some background information regarding the controversy surrounding this conflict.

While you strive to present your thesis in the most interesting way possible, try to avoid gimmicky statements, drawn-out stories or very short openings. Also avoid repeating your assignment in the introduction ("I have been asked to write about...") or beginning with an apology ("Even though it is difficult to ..."). Lead into your paper with an assured, decisive voice. Let your readers know that you are confident about your ideas. For example:

The enforcement of tough environmental laws is the only way to get rid of acid air.

The Conclusion

Just as you want to hook your readers in the introduction, you also want to leave them with a crystallized view of what you wrote—something they can take with them. Writers most often use one of four techniques in writing conclusions:

Restate the thesis—without being redundant or repetitive

Tie in an anecdote from the introduction

Suggest a course of action

End with a prediction

The first technique is to *restate your thesis* without being redundant or repetitive. You could restate the thesis about fatter Americans in the following way:

Most weight loss programs fail to acknowledge that many customers regain weight just as fast as they lose it because most dieters return to their old eating habits.

If you have opened your paper with an anecdote, you may consider *tying in the anecdote* at the end of the piece. For example, you could return to the story about the ninety-year-old woman, perhaps relating her bad dream about living in a nursing home.

A third way of concluding your paper is to *suggest a course of action*. The paper about people re-evaluating war after the trouble in the Middle East could conclude with ways people can maintain peace.

Or, you can end with a *prediction*. Regarding the statement about the thousands of trees dying you could write:

If trees thrive, on the other hand, an almost mystical contentment is sure to follow. In our minds they will rise as symbols of stability, dignity and knowledge. Their preservation will ensure our preservation.

As with introductions, there are some common pitfalls to avoid in writing conclusions. First, avoid introducing new information at the very end of the paper such as beginning a discussion about overbuilding in resort areas after you have written an entire paper about overdevelopment in metropolitan area.

By the same token, do not cut things off abruptly. As the program suggests, after a three-page essay on smoking, you cannot simply conclude with, "And that is why I dislike smoking." Avoid the long, drawn-out ending which adds nothing significant to the paper. Finally, be careful of conclusions which are too cute or too clever. Keep your audience in mind and appeal to their interests.

Remember: Do not introduce new information in the conclusion. Do not cut the conclusion off too abruptly or the converse—do not draw it out needlessly. And avoid trying to be too clever or cute. (Remember the example "Hair today, gone tomorrow"?) Keep your audience in mind and try to appeal to their interests.

"Re-vision" or "re-seeing" means checking your paper for adequate development and eliminating digressions or unnecessary information. The revision process is an opportunity to add vivid descriptions, check for factual accuracy, and write appealing introductions and conclusions. Remember *good writing is rewriting.*

✔ Self Test

From the list below, select one of the four types of introductions which best describes the paragraph:

anecdote   sharp contrast

historical information   startling facts

1. "Each spring 560,000 sandhill cranes, 9 million ducks and geese, more than 500 bald eagles, 104 piping plovers, 110 least terns and 96 of the world's remaining population of 171 whooping cranes," pass through Platte River, Nebraska. (Source: "In Nebraska: A Joyful Spring Racket." Time 5 May 1986. p. 12).

   _____

2. The process of cloning may be one of the most beneficial discoveries ever made by mankind. But cloning may lead to loss of individual rights and freedom—and to political dictatorship.

   _____

3. A beautiful day for a wedding—crisp, clear and, for Los Angeles in midsummer, relatively cool. It is a day the bride and groom would have enjoyed—were they alive.

   _____

4. "It was early morning in a Beijing park; an old man was exercising his birds by swinging their cage in his hand as he walked. The movement is said to convince the birds inside that they are free. 'We trick them, you know,' he said. 'How long can they stay fooled? Who knows? Maybe they hope. Like us. We hope. I hope. But you know in China it is dangerous to hope.'" (Source: Kramer, Michael. "Free to Fly Inside the Cage." Time 2 Oct. 1989. pp. 64-79).

   _____

5. With a little luck, the sprawling, sparsely populated country that lies just northeast of South Africa on the Indian Ocean should have thrived. It is blessed with rich agricultural lands, large mineral deposits, and untapped reserves of natural gas and oil. During the past decade, however, everything that could have gone wrong in Mozambique has gone wrong.

   _____

6. Even though Japanese imports are starting to steal the show, the small-block Chevrolet V8 is still the most common automobile engine in America. Since its debut in 1955, car owners have recognized the small block's power-to-weight benefits. Almost as soon as it was off the assembly line, enthusiasts began modifying it. Even the factory experimented by increasing the small-block's size from the original 265 inches to displacements as large as 400 cubic inches.

_____

Select the correct word and fill in the blank.

bias	slant
development	topic sentence

7. The body paragraphs of your essay are comprised of a _____ and several supporting sentences which develop that point.

8. If an idea needs more explanation or support, the problem is that your paragraph lacks _____.

9. _____ is a way of writing about something from the writer's point of view.

10. _____ is a prejudice which ignores the facts or contradictory evidence and makes a judgment based on emotion.

Check your answers at the end of this lesson.

Writing Assignments

1. Write a 250-word essay on the steps you should take in revising your writing. What problems do you look for? Where do you have the most trouble? How can you revise the introduction and conclusion?

2. Select three consecutive paragraphs from the first draft of your research paper. Revise those paragraphs by adding, deleting and moving material around until you are satisfied with them. Note all of your revisions and add a paragraph or two explaining your changes.

3. If you have prepared a conclusion to your paper, rewrite your conclusion using one of the following techniques: restating your thesis, tying in an anecdote from the introduction, suggesting a course of action, or making a prediction.

Answer Key

1. startling facts
2. sharp contrast
3. sharp contrast
4. anecdote
5. sharp contrast
6. historical information
7. topic sentence
8. development
9. slant
10. bias

Editing the Paper

Looking for Grammatical and Mechanical Errors

✔ Lesson Preview

In the *revision* stage of your research paper, you clarified and polished the *ideas* in your paper, but now that you are in the *editing* phase, you will be checking your paper for *mechanical errors*. You will review your paper to eliminate errors in grammar, usage, punctuation and spelling. This is the last step in writing your research paper. This is your opportunity to remove any rough spots and imperfections that may remain.

> Editing a paper is like applying the
> second coat of paint—it is a finishing process.

Each sentence in your paper should express a complete thought that relates clearly to the overall development of your paper. Your ideas should connect logically and be stated as precisely as possible. In the editing phase you will be looking at the mechanical aspects of your paper. You will be checking your paper to make sure that subjects and verbs agree, that comparisons match, that all pronouns clearly refer to their antecedents, and that there are no misplaced or dangling modifiers. You will also be editing for diction—eliminating slang expressions and repetitive words. This lesson will explain the most common types of mechanical errors and provide practice in identifying and correcting them. You will also learn several ways to proofread your paper.

Learning Objectives

After completing this lesson, you will be able to:

➤ Identify ways to correct errors in punctuation and spelling

➤ Recognize and rewrite sentences that lack unity

➤ Recognize and revise common writing errors including mixed constructions, mixed metaphors, lack of parallelism, subject-verb disagreement, and misplaced and dangling modifiers

➤ Identify and revise pronoun reference errors

➤ Identify examples of poor diction or the use of vague words, needless repetition and slang

► Begin to proofread for typographical errors and omissions

✔ View the Video Program

As you view the program, look for examples of regional expressions. Think about words or expressions that are common in your area that should be avoided in your own writing.

✔ Lesson Review

As you have seen, editing means eliminating mechanical errors in grammar, usage, punctuation and spelling. Just as sanding removes any remaining rough spots and imperfections for a carpenter, editing is the finishing process in the construction of a research paper. Common errors to look for include lack of sentence unity, problems with subject-verb agreement, misplaced or dangling modifiers, and problems with parallelism and diction.

Examining Your Paper for Sentence Unity

Just as you checked each *paragraph* in your paper for unity in the *revision* stage, you should examine each *sentence* for unity in the *editing* stage. Any group of words which begins with a capital letter and ends with a period should express a complete thought. You should be able to take any sentence in your paper out of the context and read it with understanding. This is sentence unity. A sentence is unified when all parts contribute to one main idea.

A sentence lacks unity if it:

    Combines unrelated ideas

    Contains so many details that the reader misses the point

    Contains mixed metaphors

    Includes mixed or awkward constructions

Combining Unrelated Ideas

A sentence lacks unity if it combines unrelated ideas. There is no apparent connection between the two ideas in this sentence:

> Our government doesn't spend enough money on defense, but many Americans will be homeless.

In this example the writer leaped from one subject, defense spending, to another, the homeless, without attempting to connect the ideas. The relationship is not clear and the point of the sentence is lost. The sentence was rewritten:

> Our government doesn't spend enough money on defense, but to spend any more on weapons instead of human services could cause many more Americans to be homeless.

Including Too Many Details

Your readers will also miss the main point of your sentence if it contains too many details. Excessive detail obscures the central thought of the following sentence:

> In 1962, after he had served 1000 days as President of the United States, during a presidency which many people referred to as a modern-day "Camelot" which accomplished many strides, including averting the Cuban missile crisis and establishing the Peace Corps, John F. Kennedy was shot and killed by an assassin's bullet in Texas.

If your sentence contains too many details, you can either rewrite the sentence and eliminate some of the details or you can break it down into several sentences. In this case the writer decided to drop some of the details and the main point of the sentence became much clearer:

> In 1962, after he had served 1000 days as one of the most popular presidents of the United States, John F. Kennedy was shot and killed by an assassin's bullet.

Mixing Metaphors and Using Mixed Constructions

Figures of speech in which you use words in an imaginative rather than a literal sense can enrich your paper by making your writing more lively and more colorful. Misused figures of speech, however, will confuse your readers and leave the main point unclear.

Two frequently used figures of speech are the **simile** and **metaphor**. A **simile** is an explicit comparison of two things using *as* or *like*. A **metaphor** is an implied comparison in which *as* or *like* is not used.

> *Simile*:   Her *eyes* are as *deep* as the *ocean*.
>
> *Metaphor*:   *Math* is a *killer*.

Her *eyes* and the *ocean* are very different, but can be compared on a common characteristic—they are both *deep*. A **mixed metaphor** occurs when you use two or more comparisons that don't share a common characteristic.

> *Mixed Metaphor*:   Playing with *fire* can get you into *deep water*.

Mixed constructions occur when you combine different parts of speech in the same sentence. For example:

> Does anyone know why Mark quit or where did he find a better job?

Avoid awkward or obscure sentences. For example:

> *It* was tiny and sparsely decorated, but *which* was liveable nonetheless.

The sentence can be revised in two ways—both of which are correct:

> *It* was tiny and sparsely decorated, but *it* was liveable nonetheless.
>
> *It* was a tiny and sparsely decorated *house, which* was liveable nonetheless.

Reading your sentences aloud will often help alert you to this problem.

Agreement

A sentence may lack unity when the subject and predicate do not fit together logically. For example:

One *article* I read *believes* in equal pay for both sexes.

The subject of this sentence, *article*, cannot *believe*; this sentence is illogical. The sentence was altered to read:

The *author* of one article I read *believes* in equal pay for both sexes.

Looking for Problems with Subject-Verb Agreement

A major problem in many papers is using subjects and verbs that don't agree in number. Students rarely make this error when subjects and verbs are near each other in a sentence. Your natural ear for language tells you that something is wrong. For example, "The clock is ticking" sounds right. The singular subject "clock" requires a singular verb, "is ticking." Many students run into trouble, however, when the subject and verb are separated from each other. "The *clock* in the house *is* ticking." This sentence has a singular subject "clock" separated from the verb "is ticking" by the prepositional phrase "in the house." When "clock" is changed to plural, however, many students are tempted to leave the verb singular because of its proximity to the object of the preposition "house." But the verb must also be changed:

Incorrect: The *clocks* in the house *is ticking.*
Correct: The *clocks* in the house *are ticking.*

Recall this example from the video program:

Incorrect: The *pounding* of the drums *make* the animals nervous.

The singular subject "pounding" requires a singular verb, "makes." Because the prepositional phrase "of the drums," separates the subject and verb, agreement is more difficult to determine. The sentence was revised to read:

Correct: The *pounding* of the drums *makes* the animals nervous.

If you are unsure about subject-verb agreement, try eliminating the prepositional phrase mentally: "The pounding (of the drums) makes the animals nervous."

A plural verb is required when connecting two or more subjects with "and." As you saw in the program, the following sentence contains two subjects—"revising" and "editing," and therefore requires a plural verb.

Revising and *editing* are important to the process of writing a paper.

Exception: When "each" or "every" precedes one of the subjects, the verb should be singular.

Each child and *adult has* his own ticket.

115

When you encounter situations in which subject-verb agreement is difficult to determine, consult a handbook for more information. Most college handbooks break down the rules into very specific and easy-to-read examples.

Looking for Problems with Pronoun Agreement

Pronouns such as *he, she, they, him, her, them, his, hers* or *their* stand for other words. Whenever you use a pronoun, make sure that it agrees with the person, place or thing (the noun) for which it stands. For example, "She is an excellent vocalist," is fairly easy to determine because we can assume that "she" refers to one female and therefore requires a singular verb.

Many people run into trouble, however, when dealing with indefinite pronouns such as: *another, anyone, each, either, everyone, everybody, neither, no one, someone* or *somebody*. These pronouns are considered to be singular in formal English and therefore require a singular referent or antecedent.

Incorrect: *Everyone* in class should study *their* notes.

Remember that "everyone" is singular and requires a singular referent, "his" or "her."

Correct: *Everyone* in class should study *his* notes.
Correct: *Everyone* in class should study *her* notes.
Correct: All *students* should study *their* notes.
Incorrect: If *anyone* needs a ride, *they* can call me.
Correct: If *anyone* needs a ride, *he* or *she* can call me.

Identifying Misplaced or Dangling Modifiers

A modifier is any word or group of words that gives information about or describes another word. Adjectives such as *pretty, clean, cold, damp* and *burnt* are modifiers. They can be used to describe nouns such as in "*pretty* woman" or "*clean* house."

Adverbs such as *easily, boldly, graciously,* or *eagerly* are also modifiers. Adverbs modify verbs as in "She won *easily*" or "He walked *boldly* into the room." Phrases such as "while enjoying lunch" or "unhappy with marriage," are also modifiers. As a general rule, modifiers should be placed as close as possible to the words they modify. A modifier is misplaced when it is placed too far from the word it modifies and the meaning of the sentence becomes muddled. For example:

The man sighted a grizzly bear *peering through his binoculars.*

Who was peering through the binoculars—the man or the grizzly bear? As the sentence is written, it is difficult to determine. The modifier was moved:

The man *peering through his binoculars* sighted a grizzly bear.

A modifier is *dangling* if the word it should logically modify is missing from the sentence. For example:

Instead of giving up, another solution was tried.

Something is missing from this sentence. "Instead of giving up" is a dangling modifier. The missing subject, "the accountant," was inserted:

Instead of giving up, *the accountant* tried another solution.

Looking for Problems with Parallelism and Diction

Parallelism

Whenever words, phrases or clauses are repeated in a sentence, they must follow the same grammatical structure. For example:

At the end of every term I *await* my final grades, I *smile or groan* after receiving them, and *then a vacation seems* necessary.

This sentence lacks parallelism.

I await...
I smile or groan...
and then a vacation seems...

The grammatical structures are not parallel. The sentence could be improved to read:

At the end of every term I *await* my final grades, *I smile or groan* after receiving them, and then *I go* on vacation.

Comparisons or contrasts must also be parallel. From the video you saw you cannot compare a gerund to an infinitive:

Dancing is harder than *to walk.*

There must be agreement—either as verb phrases or as gerunds:

Dancing is harder than *walking.*

or

To dance is harder than *to walk.*

Diction

Using good diction is being sure that you have used the proper word in the proper place. Try to use words that are fresh, specific and appropriate. Remove any slang expressions from your paper, as well as colloquialisms (regional expressions) and needless repetitions. This sentence contains redundancies:

At *6:00 a.m. in the morning*, Jane *returned back* to her apartment and found a strange object in the living room.

The sentence was revised to read:

> At *6:00 a.m.*, Jane *returned* to her apartment and found a strange object in the living room.

You know it was *morning* because it was *6:00 a.m.* and you know that when she returned to her apartment, she went *back*. These words were not needed and were therefore eliminated. This sentence was also identified as too wordy:

> *Perhaps, maybe,* the principal *cause or reason* for the delay was an abundance of complaints on the part of the students.

The sentence was revised to read:

> *Perhaps* the principal *cause* of the delay was an abundance of student complaints.

On the other hand, make sure that you don't omit necessary words.

> Rain here is as scarce as the Mojave.

Missing words were inserted:

> Rain here is as scarce as *it is in* the Mohave.

Proofreading

Proofreading is a necessary part of writing and editing. Proofreading involves looking for typographical errors as well as any other mistakes you may have missed. Several options for proofreading were suggested in the program:

- ➤ Read your paper line-by-line using a ruler as a guide.
- ➤ Read your paper backwards from the end to the beginning ignoring content and concentrating only on the mechanics.
- ➤ Read your paper aloud to a partner noting each capitalization and punctuation mark.

Proofread your paper using the method that works best for you. Many students prefer to read aloud to a partner. Because most students are more familiar with oral language, they are able to *hear* problems they may not *see* on paper. Whichever method you choose, proofreading your final draft is an important part of revising and editing. This is your last chance to catch these errors! You may think that you will never master all of the grammar and usage rules, but remember to use your handbook when in doubt.

✔ Self Test

1. Identify the one complete sentence from the following list. Capitalize and punctuate it correctly. Rewrite each sentence fragment so that it becomes a complete sentence.

   the stadium to be cleaned of all debris

   that the stadium is cleaned of all debris

   the stadium cleaned of all debris

   the stadium is cleaned of all debris

   cleaning the stadium of all debris

2. Underline the subject and verb in each sentence. If the verb does not agree with the subject, circle the verb and write the correct form in the space provided. Do not change the verb to past tense.

   a. Since it was first discovered, the frozen wastes of Antarctica has been a place of international amnesty.

   _____

   b. Existing technology of the most advanced countries are unable to cope with the harsh climate.

   _____

   c. The influence of Greenpeace, the Sierra Club and the Audubon Society help to preserve the continent.

   _____

3. Check the sentences below for pronoun agreement. If a pronoun does not agree with its antecedent, write the appropriate pronoun above the incorrect form. Draw an arrow from the pronoun to its antecedent. Note that changing pronouns may require a change in verbs.

   a. Anyone who owns a computer should try their skills at the newest video games.

   b. Video creations like Pac-Man are more complicated now, and each has their own special effects.

   c. A buyer of video games may not realize what they are actually purchasing is a home computer.

4. Rewrite each of the following sentences to eliminate mixed constructions:

   a. Some people think that being wealthy is the only way to happiness.

   b. Through sending the forms in earlier than the due date will ensure prompt service.

   c. By procrastinating all the time is no way to get a project completed.

5. Identify any misplaced modifiers (M), or dangling modifiers (D) in the following sentences. Write the appropriate letter in the space provided. Underline the modifier.

   a. The girl went to the party with the young man wearing a low-cut gown.

   b. While enjoying lunch, the fire alarm went off.

   c. The flames were put out before any damage was done by the fire department.

6. Check the following sentences for lack of parallelism. Rewrite the sentences to improve their structure.

   a. As the saying goes, vacation means no more pencils, no more books and teachers aren't around to give dirty looks.

   b. Many students have attended undemanding high schools, have graduated with little effort, and they hardly gave any thought to the higher academic standards they will encounter in college.

7. The following sentences contain diction errors involving word choice that is not fresh (F), not specific (S), or not appropriate (A). Place the letter that identifies the problem in the space provided and revise each sentence using words that are fresh, specific and appropriate.

   a. I left no stone unturned in my research on the Civil War.

   b. We stayed at the Hotel Winona on our vacation which was a classy joint costing us $300 a night.

   c. A big tree provided shade for the picnickers.

Answer Key

1. Revisions will vary. The complete sentence is "The stadium is cleaned of all debris."

2. Subject/Verb Agreement:

   a. Subject = wastes; verb = has been
   (The verb needs to be changed to the plural form—from has been to have been)

   b. Subject = technology; verb = are
   (The singular subject requires a singular verb; are should be changed to is)

   c. Subject = influence; verb = help
   (The singular subject influence, requires a singular verb; help should be changed to helps)

3. Pronoun Agreement:

   a. Antecedent: anyone; pronoun: their (incorrect)
   The pronoun should be changed to his or her

    b.   Antecedent: each; pronoun: their (incorrect)
        The antecedent should be changed to <u>its</u>

    c.   Antecedent: buyer; pronoun: they (incorrect)
        The pronoun should be changed to <u>he</u> or <u>she</u>
        Note that the verb also needed to be changed: A buyer... may not realize what he or she <u>is</u> actually purchasing...

4.   Revisions will vary.

5.   Dangling (D) and Misplaced (M) Modifiers

    a.   M <u>wearing a low-cut gown</u>

    b.   D <u>while enjoying lunch</u>

    c.   M <u>before any damage was done</u>

6.   Parallelism—Revisions will vary.

7.   Diction—Revisions will vary.

    a.   F (not fresh); area to improve: "I left no stone unturned."

    b.   A (not appropriate): terms to improve, "classy joint."

    c.   S (not specific); word to improve, "big."

L E S S O N 15

Critiquing the Paper for Grammatical Errors

✔ Lesson Preview

In this lesson you will observe a class in session as they critique a student's essay for grammatical errors. You will see how they are able to improve this essay by finding and correcting common grammatical mistakes. Before viewing the program, you may want to review the essay yourself and try to identify some of the errors in grammar. The essay, "Writing is Like a Mine Field," can be found at the end of this lesson.

Learning Objectives

After completing this lesson, you will be able to:

► Revise your paper to conform to correct grammar usage by following suggestions presented in the lesson

► Refer to the appropriate reference (dictionary or handbook) to look up words and rules if in doubt

✔ View the Video Program

Locate the essay, "Writing Is Like a Mine Field," at the end of this lesson. As you view the program, look for the following grammatical errors within the essay:

► Sentence fragments

► Spelling errors

► Errors in capitalization

► Subject-verb disagreement

► Pronoun reference errors

► Redundant words and phrases

✔ Lesson Review

Although correct grammar is sometimes difficult to use in informal conversations, it is essential when writing a formal paper. As you critique your own paper for grammatical errors, check for some of the common errors discussed: sentence fragments, spelling errors, errors in capitalization, subject-verb disagreement, pronoun reference errors and redundancy.

Correcting Sentence Fragments

A sentence fragment is a complete phrase that cannot stand by itself. It is not a sentence because it does not contain a subject and predicate and does not express a complete thought. Recall from the program, the second sentence does not express a complete thought:

It is cumbersome. Because we speak much faster than we write.

When corrected, the first sentence was joined with the prepositional phrase to form one complete sentence:

It is cumbersome because we speak much faster than we write.

The class discovered a second sentence fragment in the second paragraph:

If the wrong phrase or word is chosen. The opportunity for communication is lost.

These sentences were also combined:

If the wrong phrase or word is chosen, the opportunity for communication is lost.

As you examine the sentences in your own paper, identify the subjects and predicates and make sure your sentences express complete thoughts.

Finding Spelling Errors

Proofread your paper for simple errors in spelling. If unsure of the correct spelling of a word, check a dictionary. As you saw in the video, the writer misspelled the word *colloquialisms*. The essay also contains misspellings of the words: *vulnerable, interpretation, disposal, lengthy, manifest* and *existence*.

In addition to locating and correcting words that are misspelled, you need to check for words that are misused such as principal or principle and calvary and cavalry. Errors of this type will not be identified by spell-check options in word processing programs because they represent bona fide words in the English language. However, words such as these are commonly misused.

In the student's essay, two words were used inappropriately: *altaring* needed to be changed to *altering* and *affect* needed to be *effect*. This type of error is often difficult to discover. If unsure about the correct use of a word, check a dictionary or an English handbook.

Capitalizing Words

A number of rules should be followed for capitalization. One rule discussed in the program is that countries, or words derived from a country, should be capitalized. In the following sentence, the student failed to capitalize the word *English*:

The *english* language is a very expressive language.

The correction was made:

The *English* language is a very expressive language.

Another rule of capitalization applies to proper names. In the following sentence, the student mistakenly capitalized the word, *author*, which is not a proper name:

In writing, the *Author* may not be able to express thoughts or ideas based on common experiences.

The sentence was corrected:

In writing, the *author* may not be able to express thoughts or ideas based on common experiences.

Ensuring Subject-Verb Agreement

Within a given sentence, the subject and verb must agree. Singular subjects require singular verbs; plural subjects require plural verbs. In the fourth paragraph, an error was found in subject-verb agreement:

The *words comes* out almost as fast as we can think them.

Since the subject, *words*, is plural, the verb must also be plural—*come*. The students revised the sentence:

The *words come* out almost as fast as we can think them.

As you review your own essay, look for the subjects and verbs in each sentence and check them for agreement.

Locating Pronoun Reference Errors

A pronoun must refer clearly to its antecedent. Because the pronoun is located so far from its antecedent in the following sentence, it is difficult to tell what is being expressed:

The spoken word disappears into thin air. *Its* only record of existence is in the mind of the listener.

What does *its* refer to in this sentence—air or word? After determining the reference is *word*, the class improved the sentence by replacing the pronoun with the noun:

The spoken word disappears into thin air. The *word's* only record of existence is in the mind of the listener.

When you find sentences in which you have placed the pronoun too far from its antecedent, you can either rewrite the sentence or replace the pronoun with the word to which it refers and thereby clarify the meaning of the sentence.

A pronoun should also agree with the antecedent in number. In the following sentence, the pronoun it does not agree with its antecedents:

Idioms and *colloquialisms* do not read as well on paper as *it* sounds when spoken.

Idioms and *colloquialisms* are plural and therefore require a plural pronoun. The sentence was corrected by changing *it* to *they*. Note that the verb *sounds* also needed to be changed. To improve the sentence even more, the students changed *sound* to *do*:

Idioms and *colloquialisms* do not read as well on paper as *they* do when spoken.

Eliminating Redundancy

A well-written sentence should not contain repetitive words or phrases. The following sentence contains a redundancy:

When we speak, we easily use terms, phrases, idioms or *local colloquialisms* to communicate our ideas to the listener.

As pointed out in the program, the term *local* is understood as part of the definition of *colloquialisms*. The sentence was improved by dropping the word *local*:

When we speak, we easily use terms, phrases, idioms or *colloquialisms* to communicate our ideas to the listener.

When you critique your essay, identify areas of redundancy and omit those words that add no additional meaning to your sentences.

Evaluating Parallelism

A series of words or phrases should be grammatically equal or parallel. The following sentence lacks parallelism:

We write *to instruct, to entertain, to inform, providing* a record of passage through life.

In the program the class corrected this sentence by changing *providing* to *provide*. Further, it was suggested that the last item in the series be preceded by the word *and*. The sentence was improved to read:

We write *to instruct, to entertain, to inform, and to provide* a record of passage through life.

Checking for Omissions

Leaving out certain words in a sentence may confuse your reader. In the lesson the instructor explained that prepositions usually require objects. In the following sentence, the student omitted the object of the preposition *of*:

The communication is based on shared experiences and is constantly modified as the listener displays comprehension, or lack of, through facial expression or body language.

The sentence was corrected to read:

> The communication is based on shared experiences and is constantly modified as the listener displays comprehension, or lack of *it*, through facial expression or body language.

Correcting Punctuation

If the first part of a sentence is restated, specified, listed, or otherwise elaborated upon by the second part, you should separate the two parts with a colon. For example:

> The American flag consists of three colors: red, white and blue.

In the following sentence, the student used a comma instead of a colon:

> Writing is like a mine field, one wrong step and you're dead.

The sentence was corrected:

> Writing is like a mine field: one wrong step and you're dead.

Two independent clauses need to be separated by a semicolon, not by a comma. Recall the following misuse of a comma:

> You name it, we have a word for it.

The class corrected the error:

> You name it; we have a word for it.

Check your sentences to make sure that you have not separated subjects and verbs by a comma. Recall this error:

> The body language and facial expressions we take for granted in face-to-face communication, are missing.

Because the comma is unnecessary, it was deleted:

> The body language and facial expressions we take for granted in face-to-face communication are missing.

Unless there is an interrupting word between the subject and verb, don't use a comma between them.

Become familiar with the rules of grammar and apply them; thorough critiquing requires both skill and practice. There are other errors in the essay the class members did not discuss. Were you able to find them?

WRITING IS LIKE A MINE FIELD

Perfecting the art of written communication is not an easy task. It is cumbersome. Because we speak much faster than we write. Because of the passive nature of the printed word, a writer cannot be certain if he has effectively communicated a thought or notion to the reading audience. Semantics can play havoc with a writer's best intentions, opening the door to miscommunication. Writing is like a mine field, one wrong step and your dead. The english language is a very expressive language. Words enable us to identify, modify, clarify, intensify, and express the action and emotion of our day to day existence. You name it, we have a word for it. When we speak, we easily use terms, phrases, idioms or local colloquealisms to communicate our ideas to the listener. The communication is based on shared experiences and constantly modified as the listener displays comprehension or lack of, through facial expression or body language.

This listener-speaker interaction is crucial to effective oral communication. In writing, the Author may not be able to express thoughts or ideas based on common experiences. The body language and facial expressions we take for granted in face-to-face communication, are missing. The writer is incapable of modifying or altaring a text once it is in the hands of the reader. Each word stands on it's own, supported by the context created by the writer. It is vulnurable to the readers interapretation or misinterpretation. If the wrong word or phrase is chosen. The opportunity for communication is lost.

Technological advancement has had an indirect affect on writing as a form of communication. The majority of information needed at work and home is at one's disposel through the telephone, TV, computer and Fax machine allowing for instant information. With everything moving at such a fast rate, the individual no longer has time to plow through lenthy pieces of written communication. Succinct writing is foremost. Brevity is key to efficiently communicating in a world where time is of the essence.

Because of the time involved in expressing a thought in written form, some would argue that oral communication is much more efficient. The words comes out almost as fast as we can think them. Spoken phrases manefest themselves differently in the transition from oral to written communication. Idioms and colloquealisms do not read as well on paper as it sounds when spoken. Without careful linguistic strategies, a written idea can become cloudy and hard to follow, causing the reader's interest to wane.

With all these problem aspects to writing-why bother? We write to instruct, to entertain, to inform providing a record of passage through life. The spoken word disappears into thin air. It's only record of existance is in the mind of the listener. Ultimately, it is the written word that forever perpetuates the image created by the writer, providing a perpetual opportunity for communication. As long as their is a reader, a word can be read and understood.

Submitted by Jill Collins

L E S S O N 16

Writing for the Humanities

The Explication

✔ Lesson Preview

No matter which career you choose, you will probably find that writing is an integral part of your job. Whether it's writing a police report of an arrest, a plan for company improvements or a film director's movie script, you will find it necessary to use your writing skills sometime in your profession.

Up to this point you have been researching information and organizing your ideas from existing information in order to draw a conclusion. In this lesson you will be asked to apply some of these same skills to a different field—the Humanities. Writing for the Humanities may include writing for literature, the fine arts, music or philosophy. Most likely, in writing for the Humanities you will be asked to write an explication in which you analyze or interpret a work. An explication may be written entirely from your own viewpoint or may be based on critiques of others. In this lesson you will learn how to write an explication by following the guidelines of a critique of *A Farewell to Arms* and by critically analyzing two poems: "The Balloon of the Mind" by W. B. Yeats and "Stopping by Woods on a Snowy Evening" by Robert Frost. Both poems can be found at the end of this lesson.

You will also be introduced to a panel of experts who discuss issues and concerns unique to writing for the Humanities. You will learn how writing for the Humanities differs from the writing you do in other areas. You will also be presented with some tips on what an instructor may look for when evaluating *your* explication.

Learning Objectives

After completing this lesson, you will be able to:

➤ Recognize terminology and some of the special concerns in writing for the Humanities

➤ Describe differences between writing for the Humanities and writing a research paper

➤ Follow the recommended guidelines for writing an explication

➤ Organize your commentary in an order appropriate to the subject by allowing the work's structure to determine your organization and developing a thesis to guide your writing

129

▶ Recognize the differences among the types of papers which may be required in Humanities classes including a reaction paper, a review and a critical analysis.

✔ View the Video Program

As you view the program, look for at least three differences between writing a research paper and critiquing a work in the Humanities.

✔ Lesson Review

As you have seen, writing for the Humanities *is different* from writing a research paper. In a Humanities class you may be asked to complete an *explication*—the *most common form* of writing in the Humanities. An explication is a critique or evaluation of a work. In fine arts you may be asked to evaluate a painting by examining the artist's style, presence of symbolism or use of light and color. In literature you may be asked to analyze the meaning of a poem or comment on its rhyme or meter. Whatever the field, when writing an explication, you should incorporate your viewpoint into the analysis while maintaining a constant focus on the work.

In an explication you need to take a different approach from that for writing a research paper. When writing a research paper, you read as much as you can about a particular topic, develop a thesis, compile the information into an outline and then draw a conclusion based on the information gathered. An explication, on the other hand, is an attempt to clarify the meaning of a given work through commentary. An explication may or may not involve research.

Using Outside Sources

If you are writing an explication of Hemingway's *A Farewell to Arms*, for example, you may want to look up critical essays on Hemingway's work. You could begin by consulting general references such as the *MLA Bibliography, Essay and General Literature Index* or *Humanities Index*. From these references you may find that several aspects of Hemingway's works have already been critiqued—his writing style, his themes, his point of view and his use of symbolism. You may choose to draw on these critiques in order to clarify your own ideas. The key word here is *relevance*. Before you decide to use any outside source material for your paper—critics' ideas, historical background or biographical information— first ask yourself, "Does this information have relevance to my critique or am I just filling space?" If you decide to use the information, remember to document these sources in the same way you would if documenting a research paper.

Interpreting a Work Without the Use of Outside Sources

If you are writing an *interpretation* of a novel, then the book itself becomes your primary source and you will not have references from which to take notes or cite. In this case you analyze and comment on the work from *your point of view*—but without allowing your own opinions to take over. Use your own ideas and point of view only as they specifically relate to the work. Recall the two interpretations of Robert Frost's poem, "Stopping by Woods on a Snowy Evening":

Personal Analysis:

This poem can be thought of as a statement of man's everlasting responsibility to man; though the dark and nothingness tempt him to surrender, he will not give in.

Personal Opinion:

Almost every day we find ourselves faced with the lures of temptation... while we are in college we are often tempted to do what's easiest and neglect our studies and party. However, we know that we have promises to keep and obligations to be fulfilled.

While this analysis does suggest an interpretation of the poem, the writer has strayed too far from the original focus of the poem by infusing personal opinion.

Caution: An explication provides commentary and clarifies the meaning of a work. **An explication should not**:

➤ paraphrase the work

➤ summarize the plot

➤ include biographical or historical data unless it adds to the interpretation

Recommended guidelines for writing an explication:

➤ Integrate your viewpoint into the explication while remaining objective

➤ Clarify the meaning of the work

➤ Use relevant source material

➤ Follow the work's organization

Organizing Your Explication

A common and fairly simple way of organizing explications is to follow the structure of the work itself. To explicate a poem, for example, you can follow it line by line; you can follow a play, scene by scene. Recall Yeats' poem, "The Balloon of the Mind":

Hand do what you're bid:
Bring the balloon of the mind
That belies and drags in the wind
Into its narrow shed.

The student in the program organized her writing according to the structure of the poem:

These four lines are about writing poetry—the difficulty of getting one's floating thoughts down on paper. Line one is blunt—it is a directive to the author's hands, ordering them to do what they're supposed to do. Lines two and three ramble—like the mind rambles. These lines amplify the metaphor of the poem—that the mind is like an airy, unwieldy balloon....

Although this approach is effective and easy to follow, there are two problems to watch for. First, try to avoid repetitious phrases such as "In line one," "In line two," and "In line three." Instead, vary your language such as, "In the first stanza" or "Line one suggests..."

The second caution is to be sure you have a clear understanding of the literary, musical, art or philosophical terms you are using. When writing about poetry for example, you may want to refer to an anthology or a textbook to look up the definitions of terms such as *symbolism*, *meter* or *iambic pentameter* before using them. These books may also provide examples of explications which may be well worth examining.

When explicating a larger work, such as a novel, you should organize your writing around a thesis just as you do for an essay or research paper. The student in the lesson developed the following thesis for *A Farewell to Arms*:

> Hemingway's style departs from traditional fictional prose in that it contains simple, declarative sentences and avoids excessively descriptive language.

In writing the explication, the student can then go on to illustrate how Hemingway's style departs from others by quoting his work and by comparing his writing to other, more traditional fiction writers.

Additional Types of Papers for the Humanities

In addition to explications, a Humanities class may require *reaction papers*, *reviews* or *critical analyses*.

A *reaction paper* deals almost solely with your personal response to a work. Although you may make personal associations or comparisons to other works, remember to use specific examples from the work to offer justification and support for your responses.

A *review* takes a more objective view of a work, ultimately resulting in a critical stance regarding the work's success. It is especially important in a review to be familiar with the terminology in the field, whether it's literature, music, art, or philosophy. You may also want to read other related reviews before attempting one of your own.

A *critical analysis* resembles an explication. Some instructors may ask you to synthesize the views of the critics on a particular work, while excluding your own ideas. Be sure you know what your professor expects.

Like all other kinds of composition, writing for the Humanities requires you to be well-organized and to express yourself clearly. Some other tips for writing for the Humanities include:

1. Introduce the work adequately, giving a brief summary of its themes and providing the author's name.
2. Keep the focus of your paper on the work itself.
3. Inject your viewpoint and your original analysis, but remain as objective as possible throughout your paper.
4. Support your ideas by providing specific examples from the work itself.
5. Be familiar with the terminology in the field, but avoid using the cliches of that field.

Keeping these tips in mind, knowing the work itself, familiarizing yourself with the field's language and keeping a tight focus on the subject will all help you to write a successful paper in the Humanities.

Stopping by Woods on a Snowy Evening

By Robert Frost

Whose woods these are I think I know.
His house is in the village though;
He will not see me stopping here
To watch his woods fill up with snow.

My little horse must think it queer
To stop without a farmhouse near
Between the woods and frozen lake
The darkest evening of the year.

He gives his harness bells a shake
To ask if there is some mistake.
The only other sound's the sweep
Of easy wind and downy flake.

The woods are lovely, dark and deep,
But I have promises to keep,
And miles to go before I sleep,
And miles to go before I sleep.

The Balloon of the Mind

By W. B. Yeats

Hand do what you're bid:
Bring the balloon of the mind
That belies and drags in the wind
Into its narrow shed.

✔ Self Test

From the list below, choose the correct word or phrase to fill in the blank.

cliches   reaction paper   work's organization

explications   relevance

1. A personal response to a work or a _____ allows you to include personal associations and comparisons.

2. In organizing an explication you can let the _____ determine your own organization.

3. The key word for deciding whether to use an outside source in your explication is _____.

4. Tried-and-true theses statements or _____ should be avoided when writing a paper for the Humanities.

5. _____ include your own ideas about a work with support from the critics and the work itself.

Mark each statement True or False.

6. _____ In writing reviews you should not be concerned with the field in which the work belongs.

7. _____ Your explication will be a lot more acceptable if you include many personal stories and examples.

8. _____ It is a good idea to read sample explications in the appropriate field before attempting one of your own.

9. _____ Avoid reading critics' writing on the work you have chosen. It will either confuse you or cause you to plagiarize.

10. Read the following two examples on Flannery O'Connor's short story, "Revelation." Determine which example represents a personal opinion and which is a personal analysis.

    a. In the story, "Revelation," Flannery O'Connor implies that staunch religious fanatics lose sight of the real needs in the world because they are too caught up in their beliefs. The religious have gone overboard when they do not recognize that a poor man requires food and shelter before he can attend church regularly. Such is the case with Mrs. Turpin in "Revelation."

    b. Flannery O'Connor writes about the problem of becoming a religious fanatic like my mother. Unfortunately, my mother does not even acknowledge that poor Mrs. Bunsinger needs a roof over her own head before she can enter the House of God.

Writing Assignment

Talk to someone who works in an occupation that interests you and ask about the kind of writing that is required. Write a one-page summary reporting your findings. Include in the summary an assessment of your feelings regarding the writing requirements in that field and your academic preparation for such writing.

Answer Key

1. reaction paper
2. work's organization
3. relevance
4. cliches
5. explications
6. F
7. F
8. T
9. F
10. a. Personal analysis
    b. Personal opinion

L E S S O N 17

Critiquing the Explication

✔ Lesson Preview

In this lesson you will view a class as the students and instructor evaluate two essays on "Indian Camp," a short story by Ernest Hemingway. The class examines the essays for use of imagery, the citation of specific examples and development of strong introductory paragraphs. Two distinctly different approaches to writing are taken. In the essay, "What They Don't Teach You in Medical School," the student explicates the short story by using "Indian Camp" as his primary source. His analysis is based solely on his personal interpretation of the work. The other composition, "Nick's Fall From Innocence," is research-based and includes critiques from other critical essays to strengthen its analysis. Both are valid approaches to writing the explication. In order to better understand the class, you may want to read "Indian Camp" before watching the video program. A copy of the short story as well as the student essays can be found at the end of the lesson.

Learning Objectives

After completing this lesson, you will be able to:

➤ Discuss the differences between an explication based on research and one that is strictly interpretative

➤ Evaluate your own essay by recognizing strengths and weaknesses in your writing

➤ Improve your own explication by following the guidelines reviewed

✔ View the Video Program

As you view the program, look for differences between the explication in which outside sources are used and the explication based solely on the writer's interpretation of the work.

✔ Lesson Review

As you saw in the video, when you explicate a work from art, literature, music or any other field in the Humanities, you should accomplish the following:

➤ Compose a strong introduction

- ➤ Document outside sources
- ➤ Use examples of imagery when appropriate
- ➤ Cite specific examples
- ➤ Avoid interjecting personal opinion

Writing Strong Introductions

An introduction to any paper you write should be interesting and *hook* your readers so they will want to continue reading your work. As you saw in the lesson, Julie created a strong and effective introduction by including historical information relevant to the interpretation of the work in her essay, "Nick's Fall From Innocence":

> When Ernest Hemingway introduced the character of Nick Adams to the reading world in 1938, he created a character that became indelibly imprinted on the minds and hearts of his reading audience. "Indian Camp" was the first of a series of short stories and set the backdrop for all Nick stories to come.

Even though you have learned that explications should not include historical data, in this case the historical references were appropriate and actually enhanced the introduction. The fact that "Indian Camp" was Hemingway's first "Nick story" influences the reader's approach to the work.

Documenting Research Materials

As you learned, critical essays can provide relevant material which affects your thesis and your interpretation of the work. When you take a research-based approach to your explication, you must remember to document your sources just as you do in any research paper. Recall that Julie used an outside source but neglected to include the author's name:

> In his essay "Initiation" (from <u>Indian Camp</u> and <u>The Doctor's Wife</u>), the author claims the naming of Hemingway's character served as a literary device, typifying the entire human race who have encountered irrational elements....

Remember to include the name of the writer and the source from which a quote is taken. You should provide enough information for a reader to locate the original work.

Using Imagery

Exploring the use of images is important to the analysis and interpretation of any story or poem. An image is a picture the author paints with words—a picture which can be interpreted on different levels. Including imagery from the text helps explain the development of your analysis. Recall Julie's use of imagery to develop her point regarding Hemingway's use of light: "The light images in 'Indian Camp' further reflect that Nick is about to journey into new knowledge as he travels from darkness into light." She then provided specific examples:

> It was much lighter on the logging road as the timber was cut away on both sides. Ahead were the lights of the shanties... In the shanty nearest the road there was light in the window.

Later in the essay she included a passage with additional lamp imagery:

> Nick, standing in the door of the kitchen, had a good view of the upper bunk when his father, with the lamp in one hand, tipped the Indian's head back.

Citing Specific Examples

When using examples from the text, make sure that in addition to being specific, they support your interpretation. In the essay, "What They Don't Teach You in Medical School," Mark states that Dr. Adams has become desensitized to the fragility of his patient. He cites the lines:

> No I don't have any anaesthetic... but her screams are not important. I don't hear them because they're not important.

This example is used to reinforce the idea that Dr. Adams has become too emotionally detached to be an effective doctor.

Avoiding Personal Opinion

Avoid labeling or stereotyping characters in a work. Recall that Mark wrote that it is stressful for doctors to look death in the face every day. He then suggested that most doctors are alcoholics as a result of that stress, but he was unable to support his position with examples from the original work.

> It's no wonder that there is a higher rate of suicide and alcoholism among doctors than any other profession in this country.

Personal opinions should be avoided in explications as well as in any form of academic writing unless specifically requested.

When you write an explication, make sure you use specific examples of imagery to explain and support your position, that you omit insupportable personal opinion, and that you write a strong and interesting introduction to *hook* your reader.

Writing Assignment

Select one of the two student essays which follows "Indian Camp" and rewrite it applying some of the suggestions from this lesson.

Indian Camp

By Ernest Hemingway

At the lake shore there was another rowboat drawn up. The two Indians stood waiting. Nick and his father got in the stern of the boat and the Indians shoved it off and one of them got in to row. Uncle George sat in the stern of the camp rowboat. The young Indian shoved the camp boat off and got in to row Uncle George.

The two boats started off in the dark. Nick heard the oarlocks of the other boat quite a way ahead of them in the mist. The Indians rowed with quick choppy stokes. Nick lay back with his father's arm around him. It was cold on the water. The Indian who was rowing them was working very hard, but the other boat moved further ahead in the mist all the time.

"Where are we going, Dad?" Nick asked.

"Over to the Indian camp. There is an Indian lady very sick."

"Oh," said Nick.

Across the bay they found the other boat beached. Uncle George was smoking a cigar in the dark. The young Indian pulled the boat way up on the beach. Uncle George gave both the Indians cigars.

They walked up from the beach through a meadow that was soaking wet with dew, following the young Indian who carried a lantern. Then they went into the woods and followed a trail that led to the logging road that ran back into the hills. It was much lighter on the logging road as the timber was cut away on both sides. The young Indian stopped and blew out his lantern and they all walked on along the road.

They came around a bend and a dog came out barking. Ahead were the lights of the shanties where the Indian bark-peelers lived. More dogs rushed out at them. The two Indians sent them back to the shanties. In the shanty nearest the road there was a light in the window. An old woman stood in the doorway holding a lamp.

Inside on a wooden bunk lay a young Indian woman. She had been trying to have her baby for two days. All the old women in the camp had been helping her. The men had moved off up the road to sit in the dark and smoke out of range of the noise she made. She screamed just as Nick and the two Indians followed his father and Uncle George into the shanty. She lay in the lower bunk, very big under a quilt. Her head was turned to one side. In the upper bunk was her husband. He had cut his foot very badly with an ax three days before. He was smoking a pipe. The room smelled very bad.

Nick's father ordered some water to be put on the stove, and while it was heating he spoke to Nick.

"This lady is going to have a baby, Nick," he said.

"I know," said Nick.

"You don't know," said his father. "Listen to me. What she is going through is called being in labor. The baby wants to be born and she wants it to be born. All her muscles are trying to get the baby born. That is what is happening when she screams."

"I see," Nick said.

Just then the woman cried out.

"Oh, Daddy, can't you give her something to make her stop screaming?" asked Nick.

"No. I haven't any anaesthetic," his father said. "But her screams are not important. I don't hear them because they are not important."

The husband in the upper bunk rolled over against the wall.

The woman in the kitchen motioned to the doctor that the water was hot. Nick's father went into the kitchen and poured about half of the water out of the big kettle into a basin. Into the water left in the kettle he put several things he unwrapped from a handkerchief.

"Those must boil," he said, and began to scrub his hands in the basin of hot water with a cake of soap he had brought from the camp. Nick watched his father's hands scrubbing each other with the soap. While his father washed his hands very carefully and thoroughly, he talked.

"You see, Nick, babies are supposed to be born head first but sometimes they're not. When they're not they make a lot of trouble for everybody. Maybe I'll have to operate on this lady. We'll know in a little while."

When he was satisfied with his hands he went in and went to work.

"Pull back that quilt, will you, George?" he said. "I'd rather not touch it."

Later when he started to operate Uncle George and three Indian men held the woman still. She bit Uncle George on the arm and Uncle George said, "Damn squaw bitch!" and the young Indian who had rowed Uncle George over laughed at him. Nick held the basin for his father. It all took a long time.

His father picked the baby up and slapped it to make it breathe and handed it to the old woman.

"See, it's a boy, Nick," he said. "How do you like being an interne?"

Nick said, "All right." He was looking away so as not to see what his father was doing.

"There. That gets it," said his father and put something into the basin.

Nick didn't look at it.

"Now," his father said, "there's some stitches to put in. You can watch this or not, Nick, just as you like. I'm going to sew up the incision I made."

Nick did not watch. His curiosity had been gone for a long time.

His father finished and stood up. Uncle George and the three Indian men stood up. Nick put the basin out in the kitchen.

Uncle George looked at his arm. The young Indian smiled reminiscently.

"I'll put some peroxide on that, George," the doctor said.

He bent over the Indian woman. She was quiet now and her eyes were closed. She looked very pale. She did not know what had become of the baby or anything.

"I'll be back in the morning," the doctor said, standing up. "The nurse should be here from St. Ignace by noon and she'll bring everything we need."

He was feeling exalted and talkative as football players are in the dressing room after a game.

"That's one for the medical journal, George," he said. "Doing a Cesarean with a jack-knife and sewing it up with nine-foot, tapered gut leaders."

Uncle George was standing against the wall, looking at his arm.

"Oh, you're a great man, all right," he said.

"Ought to have a look at the proud father. They're usually the worst sufferers in these little affairs," the doctor said. "I must say he took at all pretty quietly."

He pulled back the blanket from the Indian's head. His hand came away wet. He mounted on the edge of the lower bunk with the lamp in one hand and looked in. The Indian lay with his face toward the wall. His throat had been cut from ear to ear. The blood had flowed down into a pool where his body sagged the bunk. His head rested on his left arm. The open razor lay, edge up, in the blankets.

"Take Nick out of the shanty, George," the doctor said.

There was no need of that. Nick, standing in the door of the kitchen, had a good view of the upper bunk when his father, the lamp in one hand, tipped the Indian's head back.

It was just beginning to be daylight when they walked along the logging road back toward the lake.

"I'm terribly sorry I brought you along, Nickie," said his father, all his post-operative exhilaration gone. "It was an awful mess to put you through."

"Do ladies always have such a hard time having babies?" Nick asked.

"No, that was very, very exceptional."

"Why did he kill himself, Daddy?"

"I don't know, Nick. He couldn't stand things, I guess."

"Do many men kill themselves, Daddy?"

"Not very many, Nick."

"Do many women?"

"Hardly ever."

"Don't they ever?"

"Oh, yes. They do sometimes."

"Daddy?"

"Yes."

"Where did Uncle George go?"

"He'll turn up all right."

"Is dying hard, Daddy?"

"No, I think it's pretty easy, Nick. It all depends."

They were seated in the boat, Nick in the stern, his father rowing. The sun was coming up over the hills. A bass jumped, making a circle in the water. Nick trailed his hand in the water. It felt warm in the sharp chill of the morning.

In the early morning on the lake sitting in the stern of the boat with his father rowing, he felt quite sure that he would never die.

WHAT THEY DON'T TEACH YOU IN MEDICAL SCHOOL

(Interpretative)

In the midst of embracing the principles of life and death, a medical student learns a valuable lesson which becomes the cornerstone for building his or her entire career. It is not taught in a specific class, and whether it happens in medical school, during internship, or residency is uncertain; what is certain is that it happens. At some point a doctor learns to establish emotional distance when attending to the needs of his patient, while still trying to display the compassion that human suffering deserves.

Although mankind is bombarded daily with images of life and death, none are as vivid as what a doctor encounters. People vicariously experience death as spectators of life's tragic moments. One can read about it in the newspaper or see it on TV, but seldom does it crash into one's life as a violent reminder of the frailty and mortality of man. For the most part, death keeps her distance until it is least expected. But for a doctor, she waits around every corner. She will rouse him from his restless on-call slumber only to announce she has made her final rounds. Emotional detachment becomes his greatest friend.

The doctor in Ernest Hemingway's short story, "Indian Camp," manifests the characteristics of a man who has taken detachment to the furthest extreme. Dr. Adams, along with his son Nick, journeys to an Indian camp where a squaw has been in labor for almost two days. As they

143

enter the camp, the reader can almost hear the tormented screams of the mother in childbirth as Hemingway paints the following picture, "She screamed just as Nick and the two Indians followed his father and Uncle George into the shanty. She lay in the lower bunk, very big under a quilt.... In the upper bunk was her husband."

Nick's father provides a fairly straightforward description of the pain that is transacting but it is his response to the screams that demonstrates the detachment with which he approaches his role. "What she is going through is called being in labor.... All her muscles are trying to get the baby to be born. That is what is happening when she screams." When Nick asks his father to alleviate her pain, Dr. Adams responds, "No I don't have any anaesthetic.... but her screams are not important. I don't hear them because they are not important." Not only has he become incapable of ministering to the needs of his patient (he is without anaesthetic), but he no longer sees this as his role (her screams are not important). Dr. Adams has become desensitized to the pain of his patient. His job is to deliver the baby--which he does at the greatest emotional distance possible. It has become impossible for him to display the compassion that suffering deserves.

After the Caesarean is completed, Dr. Adams is seen at his most in-sensitive moment. "He was feeling exalted and talkative as football players are in the dressing room after a game." When he says, "That's one for the medical journal, George. Doing a Caesarean with a jack-knife and sewing it up with nine-foot, tapered gut leaders," it appears that he is proud of the ruthless, raw procedure that he has success-

144

fully accomplished. The reader is inclined to interpret this as spoken with a spirit of cruel jesting. One can argue that sarcasm and jest continue to be a mechanism for maintaining emotional distance in today's medical arena.

The story takes a violent, ironic twist as the words of Dr. Adams ("...her screams are not important") come back to haunt him. After completing the Caesarean, he climbs to the top bunk to inform the husband that the surgery has been successful. "The Indian lay with his face toward the wall. His throat had been cut from ear to ear. The blood flowed down into a pool where his body sagged the bunk." The Indian, unable to cope with the intense pain and constant screaming of his wife, had taken his own life by slitting his throat, at the same time that Dr. Adams disregarded the suffering. The screams had not been important to Dr. Adams, yet they determined the destiny of the Indian brave by driving him to suicide. The husband had been so emotionally close to the screams that the only solution was to drown them out forever. Dr. Adams had been so emotionally distant that he heard them only as a faint whisper.

It's no wonder that there is a high rate of suicide and alcoholism among doctors in this country. How many other professions require you to stare death in the face everyday, while the world around you pretends life will last forever? Emotional distance is a crucial element in the performance of any doctor, but taken to an extreme it can destroy the empathic essence required of those who would effectively practice medicine.

Submitted by Mark Bowden

NICK'S FALL FROM INNOCENCE

(Research-Based)

When Ernest Hemingway introduced the character of Nick Adams to the reading world in 1938, he created a character that became indelibly imprinted in the minds and hearts of his reading audience. "Indian Camp" was the first of a series of short stories and set the backdrop for all the Nick stories that were to come. Nick Adams, claimed by some critics to be an archetypal Adam, leads his reader through a perpetual fall from innocence as he constantly encounters and responds to experiences which reflect a world of chaos. In his essay "Initiation" (from *Indian Camp* and *The Doctor's Wife*), the author claims the naming of Hemingway's character served as a literary device, typifying the entire human race encountering irrational elements in their environment and forced to reconcile them. He notes the parody of Old Nick--another name for Satan--the archetype of evil. Thus in one name, the struggle between good and evil is reflected. Nick Adams, throughout his life attempts to maintain a balance between these two elements as he encounters a series of experiences and adventures that define a departure of innocence and lead to the realization of the fallen nature, chaos and ultimate death which pervade man's existence. It is in "Indian Camp" that we see Nick at his youngest. As a result of his immaturity, he is unable to manifest an understanding of the chaotic world which he discovers at the camp and thus denies the experience that characterizes his initial fall from innocence.

We are first introduced to young Nick Adams with his father as they are about to embark on both a literal and symbolic journey in which "two boats started off in the dark" with destiny unknown. Nick is secure in both himself and his father's arms when he asks, "Where are we going, Dad?" and told, "Over to the Indian camp. There is an Indian lady very sick."

The light images in "Indian Camp" further reflect that Nick is about to journey into new knowledge as he travels from darkness into light. "It was much lighter on the logging road as the timber was cut away on both sides.... Ahead were the lights of the shanties.... In the shanty nearest the road there was a light in the window." The description of an old woman who "stood in the doorway holding a lamp" recalls the symbol of "he knowledge of good and evil" inviting Nick to enter into a new understanding of the predicament of mankind.

Inside the shanty the reader is given a disturbing picture of the madness and chaos which colors mankind's daily existence. An Indian squaw "had been trying to have her baby for two days." Dr. Adams explains, "Babies are supposed to be born head first but sometimes they're not. When they're not they make trouble for everyone." At the Indian camp the world suddenly appears out of control and no longer structured; things are not the way they are supposed to be. "The baby wants to be born. All her muscles are trying to get the baby born." Again, Hemingway gives us a devastating image of mankind's impotence in gaining redemption through the rebirth. The Indian girl needs help in delivering the child thus Nick sees his father as the deliverer, or one who can bring order out of chaos--chaos vividly punctuated by the screams of the Indian squaw.

Although the stage is set for a heroic act, it is disillusionment and despair that emerge from the series of events that follow. Nick's father, by refusing to acknowledge the human need for compassion, disqualifies himself from any instrument of salvation. "Her screams are not important. I don't hear them because they're not important." Unbeknownst to Dr. Adams, during the Caesarean operation, the husband lying in the bunk above the squaw, had been driven by the "unimportant" screams to slit his throat. Ironically, despite the father's attempt to protect Nick from seeing the dead Indian, it is Dr. Adams' lamp that introduces Nick to the concept of despair and death. The reader also discovers that Nick is standing in a doorway, a symbol of entering a new understanding should he choose to walk through. "'Take Nick out of the shanty, George,' the doctor said. There was no need of that. Nick, standing in the door of the kitchen had a good view of the upper bunk when his father, the lamp in one hand, tipped the Indian's head back."

Midway through the story, it becomes clear that Nick is too young to choose to "go through the door." He cannot accept and integrate the events that have occurred. Instead he chooses to reject this startling, disturbing world and refuses to see his father and the world for what they are. "Nick was looking away so as not to see what his father was doing.... Nick didn't look at it.... Nick did not watch. His curiosity had been gone for a long time."

Although he will never be able to erase the images, smells and sounds from his memory, Nick is incapable of integrating them into his perception of the world at that time.

Nick had experienced exposure to the brutality of a world where things are not always as they are supposed to be. He also learned what some men do when "they can't stand things." Yet the last picture the reader is presented with is that of Nick being in a state of oblivion and avoiding the reality of a non-ordered universe.

"In the early morning on the lake sitting in the stern of the boat with his father rowing, he felt sure that he would never die." As Joseph Flora points out in Hemingway's Nick Adams, from this point on he will struggle to come to grips with the idea of death--especially his own death--which he briefly catches a glimpse of at the camp, but then loses.

Submitted by Julie Flanigan

L E S S O N 18

Writing for the Social Sciences

The Abstract

✔ **Lesson Preview**

Writing for the Social Sciences includes writing for subjects such as history, sociology, political science, psychology and anthropology. The most commonly assigned writing in the Social Sciences is the *abstract* which is essentially a summary. When writing an abstract, you paraphrase a work and condense it into a significantly shorter piece—outlining the central points of a work without including your own viewpoint and interpretation. In the abstract you try to convey the message of a larger piece in far fewer words. The four steps in writing an abstract include:

➤ Listing major points of a written work

➤ Verifying your facts

➤ Ensuring that you have not drawn any new conclusions

➤ Converting your list of main points into sentences

In this lesson you will learn how to apply these four steps to the task of writing an abstract. You will also view a panel of experts discussing concerns unique to writing for the Social Sciences. You will learn how writing for the Social Sciences differs from writing for other disciplines and how Social Science instructors evaluate papers. You will also be given suggestions on what to avoid when writing for the Social Sciences.

Learning Objectives

After completing this lesson, you will be able to:

➤ Follow the four steps in writing the abstract:

  • List major points

  • Verify your facts

  • Ensure that you have not drawn any new conclusions

  • Convert the major points into sentences

➤ Apply suggestions presented by the panelists in writing an effective abstract

150

✔ View the Video Program

As you view the program, look for ideas and suggestions that will be useful to you in writing your own paper for the Social Sciences.

✔ Lesson Review

As you have learned, writing for the Social Sciences has its own set of guidelines. The most common writing assignment in the Social Sciences is the abstract. Unlike an explication in which you are expected to include your own viewpoint and interpretation, an abstract should include only a brief outline of the central points of a work. In writing an abstract, you should try to convey the message of a larger piece in significantly fewer words.

Writing the Abstract

The four steps in writing an abstract include: listing major points, verifying facts, ensuring that you have not drawn any new conclusions and converting your list of main points into sentences and paragraphs.

Listing the Main Points

To begin the process of writing an abstract ask yourself: What is the main point of the work? After reading an article regarding highway safety and immigration, main points were listed:

➤ California is trying to reduce the deaths of illegal immigrants who try to walk across interstate highways at night

➤ 71 people have died

➤ Attempts to solve the problem include:

• trimming shrubbery

• posting signs

• installing lights

Verifying Your Facts

The second step in the process of writing an abstract is to check the original work in order to verify the facts. Using the illustration of Little Red Riding Hood, you learned that it would be inaccurate to state that Little Red Riding Hood overcomes the big bad wolf. The fact is that the woodcutter rescues the girl. The facts need to be verified.

Drawing Conclusions

Since the purpose in writing your abstract is to report the original information as objectively as possible, an important step in writing an abstract is to make sure you haven't drawn any new conclusions. Using the Little Red Riding Hood example again, you learned that if you state that Little Red Riding Hood is saved and is returned home safely, you would be drawing your own conclusion about the ending. The story ends at Grandma's house and you don't know if the little girl makes it home safely or not. In writing your abstract, be sure you don't draw new or different conclusions.

Converting Main Points into Sentences

The last step in writing an abstract is converting the list of main points into sentences which form coherent paragraphs. The list of main points from the sample article on highway safety was converted into the following paragraph:

> Since 1985, seventy-one illegal immigrants have been killed trying to cross California's freeways at night. In an attempt to curb this problem, the state has begun pruning shrubbery along the road, erecting warning signs for motorists and installing lights.

Even though you are writing a condensed version of a work, you can still write in an interesting manner. Avoid short, choppy sentences. Vary the lengths of your sentences as you would in any other type of writing. You should also make certain that you change the wording from the original work to your own. In some cases you may want to include original phrasing. In these situations make sure you use quotation marks. You should, however, keep quotations to a minimum when writing abstracts.

Unique Concerns in Writing the Abstract

As you learned from the panel discussion, there are some special challenges when writing for the Social Sciences. The Social Sciences as a living science is constantly evolving. The interpretation of people and events will change as time passes. It is your responsibility to analyze critically each piece of information you read. When you evaluate information, you should ask: Does the writer have a bias? What is the purpose of the piece? In what time period was this written? Analyze and develop the information in an objective manner. To help develop your analytical skills, one panelist suggested selecting a subject and using the work of two different authors from different time periods.

Because the Social Sciences involve people, your second challenge is to evaluate people's feelings, emotions or experiences in an objective and scientific manner. As suggested in the program, if you interview someone you know well such as one of your parents, you must be objective in your evaluation—as difficult as this may be!

Selecting Sources

In writing for the Social Sciences you can use a variety of sources, such as news magazines, newspapers, journals, video tapes, historical novels and oral interviews. Contemporary communication—material written or produced during the time period in which a person lives can give you a sense about the times. Historical novels can also provide information about people or events. For example, *Uncle Tom's Cabin* and *Tom Sawyer* reflect certain truths about the African-American experience in the United States at a particular point in time. And don't hesitate to use the same source for different disciplines. One panelist suggested using the novel *Gone With the Wind* for information about the politics and economics for the time period in which the novel is set.

One source often overlooked by the novice researcher is the oral interview. Although you should be careful in your selection, you can look for someone who actually lived during a certain time period or through an event. Their information can add color and strength to your paper. Be aware that people around you can be used as potential sources of information. And as pointed out by a panelist, one day you too will be a living source of information about the people or events in your lifetime. You too are a part of living history.

Writing To Your Audience

Meeting the needs of your audience is a major challenge in writing for the Social Sciences. Because you have such a wide audience, it is difficult to educate and entertain your readers at the same time. Since many students have a tendency to use words and tone with a popular appeal, you should make a conscious effort to write more academically.

Because writing an abstract means objectively reporting the information, you should not try to write to the values or beliefs of your instructor. By developing your ability to critically analyze information, you will be able to provide enough support in your abstract for your own analysis of the facts. One of the dangers in writing to an instructor's beliefs is that you may misread those beliefs. In writing your abstract, demonstrate a certain depth of understanding and write objectively.

Criteria For Grading An Abstract

Although your Social Science courses are not writing classes, you will need to write essays which convey your ideas logically and clearly. As with any paper, your abstract will be graded on content, mechanics, grammar, research and documentation.

The most important aspect of your abstract is the content. You should be able to demonstrate that you can identify cause and effect relationships, that you can relate events of the past to those of today, and that you can present your information logically and objectively. The *way* in which you present your information is also important. Every word should be spelled correctly, and your sentences should be grammatically correct. As one panelist commented, a paper for the Social Sciences should employ good grammar and mechanics in order to communicate the content effectively and convincingly.

Any research used in your abstract must be documented to show your reader the sources you have used to support your statements. If you do not document the ideas and opinions you have used, you will be guilty of plagiarism. As one panelist pointed out, one day you may be asked to write professionally and you will have to think critically about your subject. Learn to recognize and appreciate the ideas of others and always document your sources.

✔ Self Test

Short Answers

1. What is the main difference between an explication and an abstract?

2. If a person plans to major in business, why would he or she need to learn how to write an abstract?

3. The following sentence was taken from an abstract written by a student: "I don't think the Indians should be allowed to waste the resources on their lands." Is this an appropriate statement for an abstract? Why or why not?

4. List three areas of the Social Sciences.

5. Which step in the abstracting process is left out?

> List main points of subject writing.
>
> Verify the conclusions you've made.
>
> Convert the list of major points into a coherent paragraph.

Check your answers at the end of this lesson.

Writing Assignments

1. Locate an article of interest in a magazine of your choice and summarize the article in one paragraph. Develop your one-paragraph abstract by using the four steps presented in the program.

2. Look in the *Social Sciences Index* for the area of the Social Sciences that most interests you—history, sociology, political science, psychology or anthropology. Find an article in that area and locate it in your library. Write an abstract of the article limiting your summary to one or two paragraphs.

Answer Key

1. In an explication you include your own viewpoint. In an abstract you don't.

2. Social Science courses are required in college programs.

3. It is not appropriate because it includes personal opinion.

4. History, sociology, political science, psychology and anthropology are all included in the Social Sciences.

5. Check the original to verify facts.

L E S S O N   19

Critiquing the Abstract

✔ Lesson Preview

Most of the time when talking to friends, you don't want to know *all* of the details of an event. You'd probably prefer they give you only the highlights and condense all of the other information into some shorter form. Writing an abstract is like that. Your goal in writing an abstract is to retell the information from some original work, but to retell it in a condensed form. When you write an abstract, you should attempt to restate the main points of a work and explain them by using accurate and selective details.

In this lesson, you will view a class in progress as the instructor and students evaluate abstracts written on three articles from *The New York Times* on a given day. You will see how the students summarize the main points, report the facts and use details to present their information. You will see how general improvements are made when the students are encouraged to write more objectively and precisely. The abstracts used in this lesson can be found at the end of this chapter.

Learning Objectives

After completing this lesson, you will be able to:

► Recognize weaknesses in written abstracts

► Improve your own abstract by applying the principles presented in this lesson

✔ View the Video Program

As you view the program, note some techniques that you can use to find the key points in a work.

✔ Lesson Review

An abstract should include a brief outline of the central highlights of the work. Writing an abstract involves paraphrasing a written work and condensing it into a significantly shorter piece. When writing an abstract follow these general guidelines:

► Include the name of the work you are abstracting

- ➤ Name the author
- ➤ Identify the classification or genre to which the work belongs
- ➤ Follow the structure of the work
- ➤ Survey the work to find key ideas
- ➤ Avoid repetitious phrases
- ➤ Use your own words
- ➤ Use quotation marks and proper citations when you quote
- ➤ Accurately restate the facts
- ➤ Objectively summarize the work
- ➤ Use good sentence structure

Writing An Abstract

When writing an abstract, begin by telling your readers *what you* are abstracting. Provide your readers with the following information: the source of the information, the name of the work, the author and the type of work (whether it's a book, an article or a biography, for example). As you write, allow your writing to follow the structure of the original work. As the instructor pointed out, in the film *Citizen Kane*, the main character dies in the beginning. If you were to present Citizen Kane's life from childhood through adulthood and to his death, you would give your reader a distorted vision of the development of the movie.

In all abstracts you aim to convey the message of a larger piece in far fewer words. Your goal is to summarize the main points and selectively use facts to explain the points. The instructor in the program suggested using the SQ3R method developed by Francis P. Robinson, a renowned psychologist, as a method for finding the main ideas in a work.

The first step in the SQ3R method is *survey.* In order to survey, quickly look over the chapter or a section of the work you want to summarize. Look at the chapter headings, bold face items, pictures and graphs, and any study questions. These items will indicate some of the key ideas covered in the work. By applying the survey method, you are allowing the author or publisher to help you write your abstract.

The second step in the SQ3R method is to *question*. When you question, ask yourself specific questions regarding the work: "What is it about?" "Who is it about?" "Where does it take place?"

In step three you *read* the work. Actively read short sections of the work, looking for the important ideas. The fourth step in the SQ3R method is to *recite.* Once you have read the information, try to restate it in your own words. *Review* is the last step. When you review, look over each main point and sub-point in the work.

As the instructor pointed out, you should use sentence variety to make your writing more interesting. Although you can follow the structure of the work, avoid saying, "In paragraph one," "In paragraph two" and "In paragraph three." It was also suggested that direct quotations should be kept to a minimum. Use your own words, not those of the author. If you *do* use the author's words, however, don't forget to include quotation marks.

Providing Enough Information

In an abstract you should strive to provide your readers with enough information to accurately explain the points you wish to make. Recall from the video that Anne's paper summarized three concerns on the minds of Americans on February 6, 1972. One concern was President Nixon's tax plan which contained three vital features. As the instructor pointed out, Anne did not clearly explain the features of the tax plan. One of her sentences is especially vague:

> When a certain condition was met, these proceeds were turned over to the states for financial use by public primary and secondary schools.

Although this statement may have been clear to Anne when she wrote her paper, the necessary information which would help clarify her meaning was not included. In an abstract you need to provide enough information to explain your position.

Using Specific Details

A problem you may face in writing abstracts is deciding what to include and what information can be left out. Again, you can use details to support your main points. Recall Mary's essay, "Three Events that Occurred September 18, 1967." In this essay Mary tells her readers what she is abstracting and includes the source of the information.

> On September 18, 1967, according to The New York Times, a combination of events occurred producing mixed emotions from both America and the Western hemisphere.

As pointed out in the program, Anne should have included specific details in the following statement:

> A study published showed that the corruption level would pick up, but only slightly.

As the instructor suggested, this statement could be improved by explaining what the study was about, where the study was published and who conducted the research.

Using Precise Language

When you summarize a work, use your own words to retell the information that appears in the original work. Use words that precisely describe what you are trying to say. Recall Mary's description of a riot:

> Forty-two people were killed and 600 injured in a riot that emerged during a Turkish soccer game.

The class suggested that "a riot emerged" should be changed to "a riot broke out." "Broke out" more accurately describes the action. In the next sentence Mary was asked to replace the word *substantial.*

Finally, the police and troops got the riot under control after <u>substantial</u> damage to cars and houses had already been made.

Just as Mary had explained that as a result of the riot forty-two people were dead and 600 injured, she could have elaborated on the amount of damage done to the cars and houses.

Writing Complete Paragraphs

It was suggested in the program that you follow the structure of a work when writing an abstract. Use well-formulated, logically-stated sentences and write in complete paragraphs. Recall that Mary logically and clearly explained the first story she had selected.

The first story was about why the Federal Aviation Administration needed extra funds and how they convinced the White House of their need. The Federal Aviation Administration said that they needed more funds because they feared they could not keep up with the increasing air travel in 1968. This could result in many air hazards. The extra funds were expected to be used for more efficient towers and radar systems. This improvement in technology was supposed to increase the efficiency of the air traffic controllers eight to ten percent by 1968.

In this paragraph, Mary explained what the air controllers wanted—more money for radar systems and towers—and what the effect would be if the air traffic controllers received the money—increased safety. The paragraph was logically developed. Mary used details to support her points and her descriptions were accurate and precise.

When you write an abstract, remember to accurately report the facts, use specific details and precise wording, and present the information clearly and logically.

THE TRYING TIMES OF FEBRUARY 6, 1972

On February 6, 1972, Americans found themselves confronted with three crucial issues which required both national and international attention. First and foremost, Nixon had presented America with a new tax plan. Secondly, urbanization in cities across the country had become a matter of controversy. And finally, political relations with Greece were demanding careful strategies and consideration in foreign planning.

Nixon's value-added tax proposal included three vital features: rates, proceeds and revenues. The rate of the value-added tax would be somewhere between two and three percent. Taxation would occur at each segment of the distribution process on all products and services. The second feature determined the destination of proceeds from the value-added tax. When a certain condition was met, these proceeds would be turned over to the states for financial use by the public schools. This feature included the stipulation that the proceeds from local property taxes could not be used in financing public education. The final feature of Nixon's plan involved a decrease in revenue. The assumption behind this feature was that the revenue raised from the tax would reflect a reduction because of the rebate of the value-added tax to the lower and middle classes. Revenue surfaced as the key issue concerning the new proposal.

As a result of the increase in urbanization, Americans were facing three crucial questions. Were cities across America becoming overpopulated? Although people saw over-population as a potential problem, they did not see the wide-spread effects it could have across America. If

159

there was a problem, who would be in charge of urban planning and development? The article suggested it would be a matter for regional and local governments. If urbanization became a priority, would there be an increase in violence and corruption in each respective city? A published study indicated the corruption level would pick up, but only slightly; an increase in population would reflect some statistical increase in violence.

On the international level, Americans were in the midst of imperialistic debate with Greece. The problematic situation was three-fold. The Greeks were arguing their value to America was strategic if war should resume in the Middle East. The presence of American military was disturbing the island and those residing there. They also accused the Americans of involvement in the coup d'etat. Nearly the entire Greek population felt that the American military was responsible for the coup or at least had received information beforehand and had failed to provide any warnings. Lastly, the Greeks were in opposition to the creation of the Athens regime. They felt this style of government was created, controlled, and could be destroyed by the American government should it decide to do so.

America had problems both near and far on February 6, 1972. People were reading about a new tax plan while looking out their windows into crowded neighborhoods. Internationally, the American government was accused of doing some crowding of their own. These were the times that tried men's souls.

Submitted by Anne Garcia

THREE EVENTS THAT OCCURRED SEPTEMBER 18, 1967

On September 18, 1967, according to The New York Times, a combination of events occurred producing mixed emotions from both the American and the Western hemispheres. Each of the events affected a different population and aroused a different set of emotions. One situation revolved around the aggravation that the Federal Administration experienced in their attempts to convince the White House of a much needed increase in funds to improve air safety. The following story described the feelings of fear, angst and terror that were produced as a result of a Turkish riot that broke out at a soccer game. The final event encompassed the sadness and grief that American military and families experienced as a result of two simultaneously tragic events: the crashing of the U.S. bomber into a Vietnamese bridge, and a terrorist bombing of an officer's club.

The first story was about why the Federal Aviation Administration needed extra funds and how they convinced the White House of their need. The Federal Aviation Administration said that they needed more funds because they feared they could not keep up with the increasing air travel in 1968. This could result in many air hazards. The extra funds were expected to be used for more efficient towers and radar systems. This improvement in technology was supposed to increase the efficiency of the air traffic controllers eight to ten percent by 1968.

The White House was not fully convinced of the immediate political implications that were involved if they refused to allocate the requested funds. They expressed concerns about the probability of another major accident if denied the request of increased funds for improved air safety. Statistics in 1967 showed an increase in air hazards. In the first eight months of 1967, there were ten fatal airline accidents and 217 deaths compared to the annual average of twelve accidents and 293 deaths of the previous five years. The conclusive factors in determining the decision to support an increase in fund allocations were the two separate incidents of mid-air collisions of jet airliners.

On the other side of the world, September 18, 1967, was a day of excessive brutality for many innocent victims. Forty-two people were killed and 600 injured in a riot that emerged during a Turkish soccer game. Disappointed spectators became angry to the point of no control when a soccer match did not meet their expectations. They began throwing broken bottles and sharp objects and even started firing guns. Within minutes, the riot extended into the street, wreaking havoc among innocent by-standers. The police and troops got the riot under control but only after substantial damage to cars and houses had already occurred.

The third and final story reflected a nation that continually was forced to come to grips with the loss of life during the Vietnam Era. The Air Force experienced two disasters on that day. Just seven miles from Communist China, an Air Force Bomber raiding ammunition storage areas crashed into a bridge after experiencing engine trouble. This was the closest any American plane had gotten to China. That same night, terrorism reigned, as a bomb exploded at an officer's club, killing ten men and injuring twenty-nine.

These three stories combined reflect "a day in the life" on September 18, 1967. People across the globe were experiencing the gambit of emotions. From aggravation and frustration of dealing with bureaucracy, to the fear and anxiety of chaos running amuck, to finally the sadness and loss resulting from a war that never made sense, global citizens shared in the madness of the decade.

Submitted by Mary Green

L E S S O N   20

Writing for the Sciences

The Lab Report

✔ Lesson Preview

Scientific writing, like other forms of communication, is a two-way process. Just as any kind of communication is useless unless it is received, a scientific paper is useless unless it is *received* and *understood* by the reader.

When you write a lab report, you are presenting new and important scientific information. As in all types of writing, you should phrase your information accurately and clearly. However, this point is especially important in writing a lab report since the information is being stated for the first time. In a lab report you must be able to do more than analyze a problem; you must be able to relate your findings to someone else. In this lesson you will observe an instructor as he describes the components of a lab report to his class. Later in the lesson you will view a panel of experts discussing some concerns unique to writing for science. You will be presented with suggestions that can help you produce a well-written lab report.

Learning Objectives

After completing this lesson, you will be able to:

▶ Prepare a lab report incorporating the seven integral parts presented

▶ Recognize the components of a well-written theory discussion

▶ Write a summary of procedures

▶ Complete a data sheet

▶ Write a conclusion which includes the objective, verification and interpretation of the data

✔ View the Video Program

As you view the program, look for suggestions you can apply to writing for your own classes in the sciences.

✔ Lesson Review

As you have learned, when writing a lab report, you should write as if you are trying to sell your report to your boss. You are trying to prove that you know what you are talking about by describing clearly what you found out. The information that you present in your lab report is both important and new—make sure to write clearly so that your readers will understand the information.

A laboratory report consists of seven parts. When writing your report, include the following information:

1. Cover page
2. Theory discussion
3. Summary of procedures
4. Data sheet
5. Sample calculations
6. Graphs (if required)
7. Conclusion

The Cover Page

The cover page includes the title of your experiment, the date that you conducted the experiment, your name and the names of your partners (if any).

Theory Discussion

The theory discussion is the most important part of your laboratory exercise. This includes a formal description of the physical laws that you are trying to verify, how these laws were established, and how your data verifies (or doesn't verify) these laws. You should also describe the basic hypothesis being tested. Your writing should be thorough, accurate and concise. You should be able to clearly explain the theory behind the exercise. This is not the place for, "I understand, but I just can't explain it." Take time to organize your thoughts before beginning to write.

Summary of Procedures

In the summary of procedures you should include an explanation of what you were trying to find out and an accurate account of how you accumulated your data. In this section you should:

▶ State the objective of the exercise

▶ Describe the equipment used and how it was used

▶ Describe the data and how it was used in the calculations to obtain the desired results

If the theory discussion describes *why* you performed this experiment, the summary of procedures describes *what* you did.

Data Sheet and Sample Calculations

The information to complete steps four and five are obtained in the laboratory. In order to complete your laboratory exercise you need to complete all four of the following steps:

➤ Data collection

➤ Data analysis

➤ Organization

➤ Presentation

The data sheet should include all of your data and any results that were calculated using the data. Data columns should be labeled with an appropriate descriptive name for the data item, an accepted abbreviation for the name, and the units in which your data

are presented. As you saw in the video, for the item *Length*, the abbreviation *L* was used for the descriptive name. The unit used to present the data was cm.

The data sheet should also include your sample calculations. Include examples of each type of calculation required in the process of analyzing and reducing your data. Recall the sample calculation from the video:

$$V = L \times W \times H$$

In order to determine the volume of a rectangular solid, they used the following relationship:

$$V = 4.0 \text{ cm} \times 2.5 \text{ cm} \times 1.0 \text{ cm} = 10.0 \text{ cm}^3.$$

Conclusion

The final step of a lab report is writing the conclusion. In your conclusion you should state whether or not you met the objective of the lab exercise and describe what you learned. Were you able to verify the physical laws you were investigating? If so, describe the accuracy of your results. If your results were not within acceptable limitations, you need to describe what went wrong. Were the errors the result of bad data, improper calculations or poor interpretation? You should also be able to isolate and describe the most likely cause of the errors. Your conclusion should also include an accurate interpretation of your graphs, any data trends observed, and any limitations your equipment may have had on your experiment.

Suggestions for Writing a Lab Report

In order to write any paper for the sciences you must have a good idea of the scope of the material you intend to include. In a lab report you already have that. But before you write, think about what you did to obtain your data. Be sure you clearly understand *what* you did and *why* you did it before you leave the laboratory. Make sure you understand your basic objective and the hypothesis you are testing. Write down everything that you think is applicable to what you did in the experiment. Once you have recorded all the information you think is pertinent, you can begin to think about the format and organization of your paper.

As suggested, you may approach your writing as though you are trying to sell your lab report to your boss. Or you may want to write your report as though you are giving it to someone who has never before read about the subject. Try to convince your readers that you have made an important scientific breakthrough.

In writing your first draft, you should be thorough, accurate and concise. Once your first draft is complete, read it aloud to yourself to see if there are any missing words and if your sentences flow smoothly. Remember, when writing a lab report it is not enough to analyze a problem; you must be able to relate the results of your experiment to someone else.

L E S S O N 21

Business Writing

✔ Lesson Preview

Business writing is the most common form of written communication you will encounter in your professional life. At the outset of your career, you will write letters of application and resumes; later you may need to know how to write memos, formal business letters and business reports. In the business world "time is money," so it is vital that you learn to communicate in a direct, succinct style. You must get straight to the point with a minimum of descriptive or creative flair. This lesson will provide tips and guidelines to help you communicate in a business-like manner. In this lesson you will learn about four types of business writing: memos, business letters, business reports and resumes.

Lesson Objectives

After completing this lesson, you will be able to:

➤ Select the appropriate format for writing memos, business letters, business reports, letters of application, and resumes

➤ Determine the appropriate language and style for each form of correspondence

➤ Compose a letter of application

➤ Recognize the components of an effective resume

➤ Write an explicit career objective

✔ View the Video Program

As you view the video program, look for writing tips that will apply to your career and that will be helpful when applying for a job.

✔ Lesson Review

In this lesson you saw that for each type of business writing—memos, business letters, reports and resumes—different kinds of information are required. When you need to communicate with others *within your organization*, you write a *memo*. When you want to write to those *outside* your company, you send a *business letter.* Or you may be called upon to write a *business report.* Each type of writing requires specific language and a different format.

Writing Memos

Most jobs require memos—an important form of in-house communication. If you are a nurse you may need to inform colleagues about a specific procedure; if you are an engineer you may need to write a request for new equipment.

SAMPLE MEMO:

MEMORANDUM

DATE: January 23, 1996

TO: Mary Barnes   HEADING

FROM: Tom Bell

SUBJECT: Leighton Project Committee Meeting
I have canceled Thursday's meeting since I have not
received an adequate number of surveys from which to
draw a conclusion. Let's set up a working meeting
with Lilly Beal so we can discuss a new strategy.   MESSAGE
Meanwhile, I have rescheduled the Leighton Project
Committee meeting for Thursday, February 6 at 4 p.m.
Please let me know what time is convenient for you
to meet.

TB/lc

CC: Lilly Beal

Encl: 3 copies of surveys

Note that a memo consists of two parts: the heading and the message. Include in your heading the date, the name of the person receiving the memo, your name (the sender), and the subject of the memo. A standard heading like this aids in quick and efficient filing.

   TO:

   FROM:

   SUBJECT:

   DATE:

Your message should consist of no more than one or two paragraphs and cover only one major topic. You may include professional terminology in your memo since a memo is meant for in-house use. As you saw in the program, people who work at computers understand that a "P.C." is a personal computer and a health professional knows that "I.C.U." stands for Intensive Care Unit.

At the end of the memo you may include the initials of the sender in upper case and the initials of the typist in lower case. If others are receiving copies of your memo, you may write "CC" (circulating copy) followed by a colon and the name of the person receiving the copy. By writing "Encl." (enclosure) you alert the reader to any enclosed information such as a copy of the annual report or copies of employee surveys. Use these abbreviations only when appropriate: they do not need to be part of every memo.

Writing Business Letters

Unlike the memo, the *business letter* is meant to go *outside* the company. A business letter is more formal since it represents you and your employer to those outside your organization. A business letter consists of six major parts: the heading, the inside address, the salutation, the body, the closing, and the notations.

If you are using paper without letterhead, include your address, but not your name, in the *heading.* This is followed by the date. The *inside address* consists of the name of the person receiving the letter, his or her title, the name of the business, and the complete address.

Next, the *salutation* or greeting, e.g., Dear Mr. Smith, followed by a colon. If you don't know whether the contact person is male or female, you can include their first name or their initials. For example:

Dear Jamie Baxter:

    or

Dear B. J. Smith:

The *body* of the letter contains your message. As with all business writing, your message should be short and to the point. Ask yourself, "What does the reader need to know?" Sometimes your sole purpose will be to inform; at other times you may wish to persuade your reader to take some action. Develop the content and the tone of your letter according to your intent. Toward the end of the letter sum up your recommended course of action and inform the reader when and how you can be reached for follow-up.

The body of the business letter is followed by your *closing.* You can use standard closings such as "Sincerely yours," "Sincerely," or "Yours truly." For a more formal close, you can use "Cordially," "Best regards," or "Respectfully yours." Leave four spaces for your signature; then type in your full name followed by your title. For example:

Sincerely yours,

John Taylor
General Manager

Choosing a Letter Format

You may choose from several different formats for a business letter: *block, modified block,* or *simplified format.* In full-block style all margins are flush left with no indentations. In modified block the heading and closing are indented. The beginning of the paragraphs in the body may or may not be indented five spaces. Simplified format looks similar to block except that it has no salutation or closing. Use the simplified format when you don't know the name or title of the person receiving your letter. Choosing a letter format is not always a matter of personal choice. Businesses usually prefer one format over another in order to establish a standard *look.*

Halifax Hospital
1052 Water Street
Jacksonville, FL 32207
March 1, 1994

Mr. Mark Osgood
CARE Group, Inc.
P.O. Box 5473
Jacksonville, FL 32202

Dear Mr. Osgood:

Thank you for agreeing to assist with the Health Conference on March 20. I am enclosing several brochures on the conference as well as additional materials on current trends in health care.

As we discussed on the phone, the major portion of the conference will be devoted to the speaker from Blacksburg, Virginia. The local presentations will follow. I will send you a preliminary agenda in a few days.

I look forward to working with you on this conference. I think we have all the components of a very informative and valuable program. Please feel free to call me at 359-6843 for additional information.

Sincerely,

Katelyn Mathews
Project Coordinator

KM/eb
Enclosures

120 Commerce Circle
Fairfax, VA 22058
March 19, 1996

Jim Baxter
Director of Personnel
Smith & Robertson's
125 New Eagle Drive
Boise, ID 83726

Dear Mr. Baxter:

I am writing to express my interest in applying for the management trainee position you have in the Accounts Payable Department. I have just earned my business management degree at the University of Virginia, and your job opening, which I saw advertised in the March 1996 issue of **Business Management** appeals to me in two specific ways. First, I am single and quite willing to travel. Second, I have a high respect for your company which is reputedly progressive. I would like to work for a company like yours because I would like to grow with a business in my own professional career.

As I have recently graduated, I am available to interview at any time. I can be reached at (703) 743-3434 or at the address above. Please let me know if I can answer any questions you may have regarding my resume or my qualifications. I look forward to hearing from you soon.

Sincerely,

Katie Goodman

Encl.

Writing a Letter of Application

The sample letter above is a typical letter of application. The style is direct—the writer states the position she is applying for, includes some personal information, and provides information about her availability for interviewing. You may want to research a potential employer to determine how much and what type of information you should provide. Some companies prefer personal information; others do not. When you are unsure of an employer's orientation, simply state the job you are interested in, give a brief summary of your personal background, and indicate briefly how you think your skills would benefit the company.

You can use the letter of application to include relevant information which may not appear in your resume or you can use it to highlight information. As suggested in the video program, although your resume may include dates of employment and a list of your awards, you may want to point out the total number of years you've worked in your field or give the number of awards you've received as a way of highlighting that information.

Writing a Resume

Unlike the memo and the business letter, your resume will rely less on your writing skills and more on good information gathering and presentation skills. Do not write in complete sentences, include paragraphs, or use transitions in your resume. Think of your resume as a picture of your professional and educational background. Your resume should be short, accurate and easy to read. Because resume formats differ from one profession to another, you may want to find a book containing sample resumes for your profession and follow that format.

Janice Kaiser
2020 Lanier Court
Jacksonville, FL 32211
(904) 744-2021 (daytime)
(904) 743-6820 (evenings)

Career Objective: To secure an entry level accounting position in an equipment purchasing division

Work Experience:
4/96-Present

T.J. Farris Jeweler's
Jacksonville, FL 32212

Bookkeeper—Responsibilities include balancing account books, disbursing cash drawers, making bank deposits and training personnel on cash registers

4/94-4/96

Ryan's Restaurant
Jacksonville, FL 32216

Cashier—Duties included ringing up customer bills, balancing cash register for every shift, tipping out waiters and seating customers

Educational Background:
9/94-6/96

University of North Florida
Jacksonville, FL

B.S. Accounting—Major Studies: Accounting and Marketing

9/92-8/94

Florida Community College at Jacksonville
Jacksonville, FL

Major Studies: General Courses

9/88-6/92

Fletcher Senior High
Neptune Beach, FL

High School Diploma

Other Information:

*Dean's List 3 of 4 years in College
*Vice President of Business Club
*Board Member-Student Activities
*Volunteer for Meals on Wheels

References: Available upon request

Note the placement of the name and address, the specific headings, the concise wording and the clear format. A college address should be included if it is different from your home address. Include your day and evening phone numbers as well.

The *Career Objective* is a one-sentence statement of your professional goals—it indicates your desired career direction. Think of your career objective as a thesis statement; make sure that it's not too vague or too limiting. The objective in the sample resume identifies a general category (accounting) which is then narrowed to a specific area (equipment purchasing). Recall from the program the student first stated a general career objective:

To get a job in the field of nutrition

She revised her objective to:

To oversee menu-planning and food preparation in a large institutional environment.

The next section of your resume can begin with either your educational background or your work experience—whichever is more relevant to the position you seek. If school has more adequately prepared you for the desired position, list education first.

Under the heading *Educational Background* list all the schools you've attended beginning with the most recent and ending with high school. Do not include grammar or elementary schools. For high school and college, include dates of attendance, your major and minor areas of study, and the degrees you have received or expect to receive.

Under *Work Experience*, begin with your current or most recent job and work back. List the dates of employment, including the month and year you began and left. Include your job title, the name and address of the company, and a brief description of your responsibilities. Each section should be no longer than a paragraph. Use sentence fragments which begin with action verbs to describe your responsibilities. Just as key points in an essay should relate to your thesis, the work experience in your resume should relate to your career objective.

Under the heading *Other Information* list any awards, scholarships and honors you've received, as well as any organizations or extracurricular activities in which you've been involved. Limit your list to those kinds of activities that reinforce your career objective. Don't try to pad your resume by listing any organization you've ever joined. Employers can tell if you're trying to fill your resume with extraneous information.

For *References*, provide the names, titles, affiliations, addresses and phone numbers of those who can speak for your abilities and potential. But before listing anyone as a reference, contact that person as a courtesy. You may choose to tailor your list of references to each job to which you apply. Some references can give better recommendations for your work experience, others can speak more to your career interests, and still others know more about your academic abilities.

Writing a Business Report

Once you secure a position with a company, you may find yourself writing a business report. Whether you are asked to write a report about personnel needs in your department or a monthly report outlining your personal accomplishments, the task will resemble the process for research writing—you'll need to gather information from some outside source, compile the information and prepare a written statement.

In writing this report start by stating the problem you researched and its significance to your organization. Also provide your readers with some background information, informing them of the necessity of the study. You may want to include in-house or important national statistics to grab your readers' attention.

Once you begin writing the body of the report, organize the content by headings. You can either present the information without commentary or you can go one step further and interpret the information for your readers and offer your recommendations. Format depends upon the type of report you've been asked to write. Business reports are sometimes written in narrative form as in the case of social workers or police investigators. Most employers have specific guidelines for writing a business report which should be followed closely.

Whatever your career choice, you will at some time be required to write memos, business letters, resumes and reports. The tips provided in this lesson and the guidelines you learn in the business world will combine to make you a successful business writer.

✔ Self Test

Choose from the following list and write the correct word or words in the blank.

action verbs	"in-house"
letter of application	most recent
cc:	narrative
colon	professional goals
Encl.	subject
flush left or left justified	inform

1. The heading of a memo consists of four items: the date, the name of the person the memo is going to, the person the memo is from, and the _____.

2. Because a memo is intended to be read _____, abbreviations and specific terminology can and should be used.

3. To indicate whether copies have been sent to anyone other than the addressee, use the abbreviation _____ in a notation at the bottom of the page.

4. Like the informational essay, the purpose of a business letter is to _____.

5. As you begin to look for a job, the first type of business letter you will write is a _____.

6. The salutation of a business letter is followed by a _____ rather than a comma, which is used in less formal letters.

7. In full-block style, everything is typed _____.

8. The career objective of a resume allows an employer to assess your _____.

9. When listing education and work experience on a resume, always start with the _____.

10. On a resume, when describing your responsibilities for a particular job, your sentences should be fragments which begin with _____.

11. Some business reports are purely informational, in some you may be asked to interpret information and offer suggestions, and some are written in first person and are more _____ in form.

12. The abbreviation _____ may be used to indicate enclosures with your business letter or memo.

Check your answers at the end of this lesson.

Writing Assignments

WRITING MEMOS

1. A new accounting firm has decided to begin advertising for the first time. As the firm's advertising director, it is your job to develop an advertising program. Before you begin the project, you decide that you would like to talk with each of the firm's ten accountants to get their ideas about the best way to advertise the firm. Your firm's name is Smith and Lopez. Compose a memo to be sent to each of the accountants.

2. You are one of the accountants mentioned in the previous assignment. Write a memo to the advertising director explaining that you will be able to meet on Monday afternoon or Tuesday morning in your office. You have several ideas for the ad campaign that you want to discuss. Your name is Mr. (or Ms.) D. Bridges and your office is Suite 112.

WRITING LETTERS

3. As a recent graduate of Florida State University in Tallahassee, Florida, you have just been hired by Express Insurance Company. You are the Assistant Personnel Director and work in the home office in Jacksonville, Florida. You have decided to apply for a Redi-Bank Credit Card through Florida Union Bank. You have filled out an application for the credit card and would also like to request that a savings account be opened in your name. Write a letter to accompany your application making this request. Address your letter to: Ralph Anderson, Redi-Bank Credit Card Department, Florida Union Bank, 1311 Pinewood Street, Jacksonville, Florida 32211.

4. Two weeks ago you purchased a new 10-speed Racer Model Lancer bicycle from Lancer Bikes Unlimited in Orlando, Florida. You have since moved to Miami and have discovered that the front brake assembly is defective. Lancer bicycles are not sold in Miami so you need to write a letter to the dealer in Orlando requesting that a new brake assembly be sent to you. You are including the defective brake assembly and a copy of the sales receipt. Address your letter to: Lancer Bicycles Unlimited, 1212 Mercer Way, Orlando, Florida 32086.

PREPARING A RESUME

5. Clip a promising job advertisement from the newspaper and prepare a resume of your qualifications to meet the requirements of the job.

    or

    If you already have a resume, submit it to your instructor for feedback on its effectiveness.

6. Write a letter of application to accompany the resume you prepared in Assignment Five.

Answer Key

1. subject
2. "in-house"
3. cc:
4. inform
5. letter of application
6. colon
7. flush left or left justified
8. professional goals
9. most recent
10. action verbs
11. narrative
12. Encl.

L E S S O N 22

Writing the Essay Exam

✔ Lesson Preview

In all of your classes you have probably been taught that organization is important for any writing assignment. But when it comes to taking an essay exam, many students seem to rely more on inspiration and luck than on their organizational skills! The planning phase of essay exams, however, is just as important as the planning phase for writing a research paper or any other kind of writing assignment. Planning *before* and *during* the essay exam can save time—time that is very precious when writing under pressure.

In a timed writing exam you are expected to recall information, present the information in a logical and organized fashion and draw conclusions based on that information. The difference from other kinds of expository writing of course is that you are working within the constraints of a limited amount of time. Even though you are not asked to answer factual multiple choice questions, you *can* and *should* prepare for an essay exam.

In this lesson you will learn how you to prepare to take an essay exam. You will learn some note-taking and outlining tips that will help you organize your thoughts before the exam. And you will learn to budget your time during the actual exam so that you don't end up with two questions to answer and no time for writing! You will also learn to look for *strategy terms*—what they are and how they should be used to determine your writing approach.

Learning Objectives

After completing this lesson, you will be able to:

- ➤ Prepare for an essay exam by following suggested tips
- ➤ Recognize and define selected *strategy terms*: define, analyze, compare and contrast, describe, evaluate, explain, and summarize
- ➤ Plan your essay by preparing an outline
- ➤ Plan for the maximum use of your time during the exam
- ➤ Evaluate and edit your essay

✔ View the Video Program

As you view the program, look for ways to plan your time during the exam so that you can spend an adequate amount of time on each essay question.

✔ Lesson Review

As you have seen, there is much more to taking an essay exam than simply writing in class. Organizing your thoughts before you write can save you considerable time and improve your overall effort.

Preparing For the Essay Exam

As is true for any test you take, you can and should prepare for an essay exam. Take good notes during class and from your reading assignments; review and outline your notes periodically. If you keep up with your note-taking, you will be much better prepared for the exam. When the time for the test approaches, make detailed outlines based on your notes. Try to determine which points have been stressed and repeated most often in class. Are there any recurring themes? Is there a thread that ties all the major points together? Write down several possible test questions and try to answer at least one of the questions before the exam to practice your test-taking skills.

During the exam take time to prepare each answer. Begin by reading *all* of the questions. If you have several questions from which to choose, answer only the required number. Devote the appropriate amount of exam time to your answers according to the point value of the questions. For example, on a 100 point exam, a 30-point question should be allotted one-third of the exam time since it is worth approximately one-third of the grade.

Identifying Strategy Terms

It is important that you know what you are being asked to do in a question. Look for the *strategy term*—the word or phrase which tells you how to approach the task of writing. Words such as *define, analyze, compare* and *contrast, describe, evaluate, explain* and *summarize* are fairly common *strategy terms*.

When asked to *define* something, you are being asked to mark its limits or determine the essential qualities and characteristics. As you saw in the program, when asked to define the runaway problem in America, the student generated the following ideas: the extent of the problem, characteristics of those who run away, and reasons for running away. The student composed the following opening paragraph:

> More than one million children in America run away from home each year. These children come from all sorts of homes and backgrounds—from upper-middle class to poverty-level housing projects. The problem crosses all income and racial barriers. Experts say the problem is reaching epidemic proportions.

The essay could then go on to define the various kinds of runaways, listing the characteristics of runaway children and describing their qualities.

Although several different approaches to writing can be taken, remember to be guided by the strategy term in the question. *Defining* the runaway problem in America is very different from *analyzing* it.

When you are asked to *analyze* a problem, you should divide the topic into categories and examine each aspect of the problem one at a time. The following categories were suggested to analyze the runaway problem:

The size and extent of the problem

The possible effects of life on the street

The problems social agencies which deal with runaways must face

Attempts to solve the problem

Note that when *defining* a problem, you do not need to examine solutions or look at courses of action. When you *analyze* a problem, however, you should separate the issues such as possible solutions or barriers to success in your discussion.

When asked to *compare* and *contrast*, *you* should show similarities and differences between two or more events or topics. For example, you could be asked to compare and contrast the runaway problem in America with the runaway problem in Japan. Or, as you saw in the program, you could be asked:

Compare the portrayal of the South in *Gone With the Wind* to that in *The Red Badge of Courage.*

The term *describe* asks you to detail an event, person or process in a way which creates a clear and vivid image. For example, you could be asked to describe the process of photosynthesis or describe the collapse of the Berlin Wall. In the program a description of the protagonist in *Gone With the Wind* included a detailed description of Scarlet O'Hara— her physical appearance, an account of her personal qualities, how she changed, her various relationships, etc.

An *evaluation* requires you to make a judgment about the value or significance of a topic. As you learned in the lesson, to evaluate the contribution of black twentieth century writers to modern literature, you could name authors such as Zora Neale Hurston or Langston Hughes and consider the effect their writings have had on modern life. In your essay you should not limit your discussion to description and definitions; evaluations require you to draw conclusions.

When you are asked to *explain* something, you have to clarify the term or the concept by using examples or reasons. You may define how it works or why it exists. For example:

Explain the increased number of teenage suicides in recent years.

In order to *summarize* a topic, you should outline the major points in a short but thorough manner. For example:

Summarize the reasons animal rights groups are opposed to animal research and experimentation.

In an attempt to answer this adequately, you could list several reasons why these groups are opposed to research and experimentation and then explain them completely.

While you should provide specific details in your answers, don't include irrelevant information just to pad your answer. For the previous example, it would be a waste of time to discuss protest strategies when the assignment was to summarize the reasons for these groups' opposition.

The answers to different strategy terms may overlap. *Explain* and *describe*, for example, are very close. Explaining involves providing reasons, whereas describing requires only details to create a picture.

> *Caution*: Always be sure you are answering the question that is asked. Remember to refer to the question as you write.

Identifying Your Topic

Before you begin to write, examine the question to find your topic. Recall the following essay question:

> Discuss the function of the river in *Heart of Darkness*.

Since the topic is "the function of the river," this is what should be discussed—not the plot of the book or the characters in the story.

Planning Your Essay

Once you understand what you are being asked to do, you should spend about 10% of your time planning your essay. Prepare a quick outline by jotting down important points and subpoints.

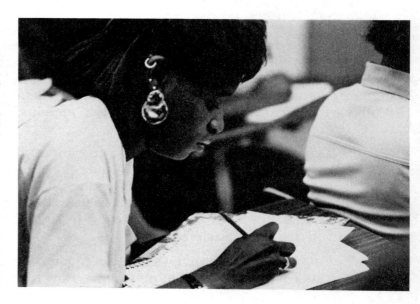

Developing Your Outline

One approach to begin your outline is to make a list of the main points you plan to cover in your essay. Then, fill in this list with supporting examples. Recall the exam question:

> *Identify* the *primary symbolic functions* of Hester Prynne's daughter, Pearl, in *The Scarlet Letter*.

The student's list included:

➤ She symbolizes the illicit love between Hester and Dimmesdale

184

- She symbolizes Hester's sin
- For Dimmesdale she stands as a symbolic conscience of the act he committed and won't admit

The student supported the first main point with the example of all three characters holding hands on the scaffold with Pearl in the middle as the link between Hester and Dimmesdale. The second and third points also were supported by examples. The examples you plan to include should be noted in your outline before you begin writing the essay.

Formulating Your Thesis

After you have developed an outline, you can formulate your thesis. This approach is different from the way you normally write an essay in which you develop your thesis first. In the lesson, the student introduced her thesis in the following manner:

In *The Scarlet Letter* the character of Pearl functions on at least three symbolic levels....

Writing the Essay

Once you are ready to write, keep the following points in mind:

- Clearly announce your thesis and establish the essay's structure
- Be direct and to the point
- Provide examples and clear explanations, avoiding digressions and generalizations
- Do not restate the questions in the essay
- Follow your outline closely
- Use transitional phrases to get from one point to another
- Write neatly and leave room for editing corrections

Remember to save some time for revising and editing your answers. Follow the same guidelines as you would for any paper. Helpful questions include:

- Does the thesis answer the question on the exam?
- Is the thesis clearly stated?
- Have all the major points been covered?
- Are the details specific?
- Is each sentence complete?
- Are the spelling and grammar correct?
- Is the writing legible and neat even with cross-outs and inserts?

The strategies presented in this lesson will help you deal with the pressure of writing with a time limitation. Of course besides knowing essay exam strategies, you must know the subject on which you are being tested. The more essays you write, the better you will become.

✔ Self Test

Evaluate the following essay exam strategies as either *Effective* (E) or *Not Effective* (NE).

1. _____ In response to a question which uses the strategy term *evaluate*, the student writes down everything he or she remembers regarding the topic.

2. _____ The student predicts several essay questions before the exam and practices by preparing answers to them.

3. _____ The student begins answering the first question he knows without wasting time reading the rest of the questions.

4. _____ The student spends one-third of her time writing an answer which counts for a little over 30% of the grade.

5. _____ The student devises a time line for answering the questions on the exam.

6. _____ The student spends his planning time writing a thesis and then tries to write an answer without an outline.

7. _____ To make her essay more interesting, the student includes a lot of personal examples to liven up the writing.

8. _____ The student fills in subtopics on his outline because he still has five minutes left for planning according to his timeline.

9. _____ Since listing works better for a student than outlining, she sticks to it when preparing to write her answers to an essay exam.

10. _____ In a compare and contrast question, the student lists and describes similarities between the two subjects.

Writing Assignments

1. Read over your notes from this class or another class you are taking. Prepare a sentence outline of the content of the course.

2. Compose three possible essay questions based on your outline above. Use at least three different strategy terms.

3. Practice taking an essay exam by writing an answer to one of the questions. Remember to outline, revise and edit your answer.

Answer Key

1. NE
2. E
3. NE
4. E
5. E
6. NE
7. NE
8. E
9. E
10. NE

Writing About Literature

Interpreting and Explaining

✔ Lesson Preview

Writing about literature involves many of the same basic strategies as writing in any field—choosing a topic, narrowing your topic and developing a well-formulated thesis. Literature, however, does present several additional challenges. Unlike most other types of writing, literature is not limited to informing the reader, like textbooks or newspapers. Because literature is primarily an art form, it can reflect and affect the full range of human experience—from anger and love, to pity and horror. Writing about literature then involves more than summarizing what happens you must explain and interpret the work.

In this lesson you will learn that in order to read and appreciate literature, you must become involved with it. You will be presented with passages to paraphrase and shown some basic elements of literary works to analyze. You will learn how to analyze character and you will learn about point of view or the manner in which an author *throws* his voice. The short story, "The Vessel of Wrath," by Somerset Maugham is used throughout the lesson to illustrate points. References are also made to *The Scarlet Letter* and *For Whom the Bell Tolls.* If not already familiar with these works, you may want to review them before viewing the lesson.

Learning Objectives

After completing this lesson, you will be able to:

- ▶ Actively read works of literature by making notes and paraphrasing

- ▶ Recognize the difference between an interpretation and a summarization of a literary work

- ▶ Limit a topic in order to provide an in-depth interpretation

- ▶ Recognize a thesis statement developed around the element of characterization

- ▶ Recognize the necessary components of character analysis

- ▶ Identify *types* of characters (stock, round, flat, dynamic and static)

- ▶ Identify the author's point of view (first person, third-person omniscient, third-person limited omniscient, third-person objective and stream of consciousness)

▶ Describe point of view by explaining the language used and how events are interpreted

✔ View the Video Program

As you view the program, identify different types of characters. Think about the various ways they can be classified.

✔ Lesson Review

The first step in writing about literature is learning how to read and appreciate it. Unlike news stories which may be composed on the spot, a literary work may take years. It is reported that Ernest Hemingway rewrote the last page of his novel *For Whom the Bell Tolls* twenty-three times! In order to treat a work of literature fairly, you must spend time with it.

Actively Reading Literature

To understand literature, you must become involved with it. Read with pen in hand, jotting down key passages and keeping track of your own thoughts. When you finish reading a story or chapter, try paraphrasing what happened—paraphrasing is one of the oldest and most useful techniques for aiding comprehension. Ask yourself: What is the mood? What is happening? Who is the main character? Rushing through a work of literature is like jogging through an art museum—you get little more than a rough idea of what is there. Take your time and think about what you are reading.

By your second or third reading you'll begin to understand how the writer has shaped various elements to form the total effect. At this point you can go beyond mere summarization; you can begin to *interpret* the work. All works of literature contain basic elements that can be analyzed. The various elements can be used to develop a focus for your writing.

Writing About Character

Character is one of the most important elements in literary works. Almost all literary works—novels, short stories, plays, and most poems—are written about characters of one kind or another. Try to identify the main qualities of the characters you read about. For example, are they greedy, naive, courageous? Do they change during the story? Is there some conflict that the character must resolve? If you can answer any of these questions, you probably have the basis for a paper analyzing character.

Types of Characters

There are several ways of categorizing characters. A complex, multidimensional character is referred to as *round*. Often the protagonist or main figure is a round character, such as Ginger Ted in "The Vessel of Wrath." Minor characters about whom you know very little and that appear to be one-dimensional are *flat*. As you learned in the program,

Dimmesdale in *The Scarlet Letter* can be described as a flat character—as is the missionary brother in "The Vessel of Wrath."

Characters who *grow up* or learn something about themselves or life are known as *dynamic*. But if no such change takes place and the characters remain as they were in the beginning of the story, they are *static*.

If a character is a type that turns up in many different stories, i.e., a stereotype, that character is considered a *stock* character. Stock characters represent a set of people—the "glamour girl" for instance, the "wealthy snob," the "good ol' boy" or the "hard-boiled detective."

Analyzing Characters

How do you determine what a character is like? Where can you look to find evidence to support your initial impressions? A good place to start is with the *physical description*. Examine the description of the character. What does the person look like? What is she or he wearing? Try to determine if there is any relationship to other, less tangible qualities. Recall the following description of Miss Jones from Somerset Maugham's "The Vessel of Wrath":

> Miss Jones was a woman of hard on forty. (Nothing in her appearance would have prepared you for such determination as she had just shown.) She had an odd drooping gracefulness, which suggested that she might be swayed by every breeze; it was almost an affectation; and it made the strength of character which you soon discovered in her seem positively monstrous....

Another way characters are revealed is through their *speech*. Use bits of dialogue in your discussion to show that a character exhibits a certain trait. Ask yourself: *How* was something said? *What* was said? *Why?* Also, look at what a character actually does—his or her *actions*. By providing examples of specific incidents that may suggest that a character is kind or cruel, for example, you can look beyond the surface to determine what the character is like. Be aware, however, that actions sometimes contradict descriptions.

You can also analyze characters by examining their *created environments*. In your analysis look for clues about where a character lives or how a room is decorated as evidence of a particular trait. Also look carefully at *what others say* about a character. Characters may have their own views about each other; use this information to help you in your analysis. By balancing all these attributes against each other, you can develop a clear picture of who a character is, and you will have plenty of evidence to support your thesis.

Determining Point of View

Don't confuse the characters in the story with the author. All characters, even those that tell their own story in first person, are creations of the author. Just as a ventriloquist *throws* his voice to his dummy, an author *throws* his voice into the mouths of his characters. This is *point of view*. The perspective from which a story is told makes a big difference; analyzing this feature can help you move beyond the surface or literal level of a work. To write about point of view, look at how language is used and how (through whose eyes?) events are interpreted.

Point of view may be classified in five ways: first person, third-person omniscient, third-person limited omniscient, third-person objective and stream of consciousness.

A story told from the *first-person* point of view uses the pronouns *I* and *we*. It is a first-hand account told by one of the characters.

Third-person views are the most common and all characters are referred to as *he* or *she*.

The *third-person omniscient* view knows everything everyone is thinking and what events will happen before they occur. The narrator often addresses readers directly and interprets events for them. The *third-person limited omniscient* view describes the thoughts of only one character. The *third-person objective* sees events as if they were recorded with a camera. There is no interpretation or entering characters' minds.

Stream of consciousness is a description of *what* a character thinks as well as a record of *how* that character thinks. Fragments of thoughts, sensations, memories and emotions are merged together to imitate the thought process in stream of consciousness.

If you can relate the use of a particular point of view to the main point of a story, you have the basis of a paper analyzing point of view. Ask yourself: What is it about the point of view that is especially appropriate to the work? Develop your essay by looking for evidence in the work that supports your thesis.

When you read and write about literature, remember these key points:

➤ Read actively and paraphrase what you've read.

➤ Narrow the focus of your subject to provide an in-depth analysis.

➤ Use the elements of character and point of view to strengthen your thesis.

➤ Use specific details of a work to provide evidence for your thesis.

➤ Interpret a work, don't just summarize it.

✔ Self Test

From the following list identify the point of view in the following passages:

a. first-person

c. third-person objective

b. third-person omniscient

d. stream of consciousness

1. _____ I had seen pictures of cowboys in books and magazines, and this fellow didn't exactly look like a cowboy. I mean, he wasn't dirty, didn't have on spurs or cowhide chaps or a red bandanna around his neck, and didn't carry a lasso. He looked like he'd just had a bath and a shave, and he was wearing an expensive black suit. But he was a cowboy, all right. I knew by the high-heeled, tooled-leather boots, the big white felt hat, and the pistol in a holster on his hip. When a Cold Sassy man carries a pistol, he straps it across his chest under his shirt and you don't see it

Source: Burns, Olive. *Cold Sassy Tree.* New York: Dell, 1984. (136)

2. _____ He loved the particulars of all this: The classic simplicity of the Underground map, with its geometric patterns and vari-colored arteries. The warm, stale winds that whipped through the cream-and-green-tile pedestrian tunnels. The passengers—from skinheads to pinstripers—all wearing the same mask of bored and dignified disdain.

When the train stopped at Hampstead, his next route was indicted by a sign saying WAY OUT, a nobler phrase by far than the bland American EXIT. Since Hampstead was London's most elevated neighborhood, the lift to the street was London's deepest, a groaning Art Nouveau monster with a recorded voice so muted and decrepit ("Stand clear of the gate," it said) that it might have been a resident ghost. He remembered that voice, in fact, and it gave him his first shiver of deja vu.

Source: Maupin, Armistead. *Baby-Cakes.* New York: Harper, 1984. (130)

3. _____ The man went into the kitchen and came out with a blue plate of biscuits. He handed them around. There's probably some molasses another man said. He talked like the field hand. Another said Check the smokehouse. They got two hams from the smokehouse and put them into a wagon and then they drank directly from the well bucket without using the ladle.

They went back into the smokehouse and brought out a barrel of molasses and put that into the wagon.

Caroline and the family came back from the fields. Vera carried William who was Caroline's youngest in a basket. They stared at the men and passed slowly into the house. The soldiers paid them little mind. Caroline came back out to stand on the back porch for a few minutes looking at the soldiers. They sat around a fire they'd built in the yard. Then she walked by them to the kitchen. Their heads turned. One said something and a knot of about four of them laughed loudly.

Source: Edgerton, Clyde. *The Floatplane Notebooks*. Chapel Hill: Algonquin, 1988. (101-102)

4. _____ My God the cigar what would your mother say if she found a blister on her mantel just in time too look here Quentin we're about to do something we'll both regret I like you liked you as soon as I saw you I says he must be a damned good fellow whoever he is or Candace wouldn't be so keen on him listen I've been out in the world now for ten year things don't matter so much...

Source: Faulkner, William. *The Sound and The Fury*. New York: Random, 1929. (135)

Evaluate the following writing strategies as either *Effective* (E) or *Not Effective* (NE).

5. _____ When asked to complete a writing assignment analyzing Jim's character in *Huckleberry Finn*, the student writes a detailed summary of what happens to Jim and Huck as they float down the Mississippi River.

6. _____ In his character analysis of David Copperfield, the student compares David's physical appearance to Dickens' appearance as a young child.

7. _____ The student carefully ensures that she separates her comments about the author from those about the speaker of a poem.

8. _____ The student reads a short story carefully one time through before he begins his analysis.

Check your answers at the end of this lesson.

Writing Assignments

1. Write a 250-word paper describing your house or apartment focusing on details that reveal something about who you are.

2. Write a page describing your own physical appearance. Although you should describe *only* your physical appearance, do so in a way that conveys something about your character.

3. Rewrite either 1 or 2 above from the perspective of someone with a very different point of view (for 1, perhaps a realtor, interior decorator or a parent; for 2, perhaps a close relative or a small child).

Answer Key

1. a
2. b
3. c
4. d
5. NE
6. NE
7. E
8. NE

Looking for Patterns
in Literature

✔ Lesson Preview

Like good screenplays, literary works use every detail for a purpose; diverse elements are weaved together to form an artistic whole. To write about literature you need to understand the way individual elements of a piece contribute to that whole. With poetry you may need to give careful consideration to each word. With stories and plays you can analyze the larger elements such as character and point of view. In this lesson you will learn about the basic elements of setting, plot, theme, foreshadowing, figurative language and symbolism. You will also learn to evaluate these elements so that you can identify patterns in a work and go beyond the surface level of a literary piece to interpretation.

Learning Objectives

After completing this lesson, you will be able to:

► Look for patterns in literature by analyzing the setting, the plot and the theme of a work

► Discuss plot and the plot line by considering causality, conflict and climax

► Identify the protagonists and antagonists in a story

► Recognize the use of flashbacks and foreshadowing

► Identify a work's theme by examining a story's conflict and resolution

► Use specific examples of setting, plot, character and theme to support your thesis

► Look for a work's deeper meaning by analyzing the author's use of imagery, symbolism and figurative language

✔ View the Video Program

As you view the video, note the settings of the various examples cited. Think about the possible purposes for the settings used.

✔ Lesson Review

As you learned in the program, to be an active reader of literature, you must become a *pattern perceiver*—that is, you must constantly look for ways the individual elements combine to produce a desired effect and contribute to the whole. Authors create patterns and weave them together into short stories, novels, plays and poems. Even though these literary forms are very different, they are composed of the same literary building blocks.

Identifying the Elements of Literature

Setting

Setting is an element of literature that authors use for specific purposes. The setting or environment provides an atmosphere—it's the world in which the characters move. In a narrow sense the setting is the physical environment—the type of house, the landscape, the location or the climate. But in a broad sense, settings may also include a point in time. As you examine the setting, ask yourself why the author chose one certain location or time period over another. Does the setting serve a purpose? Does it help reveal character? In order to answer these questions, look carefully at how the setting is described. As mentioned in the program, Christmas is a perfect setting in time for a conflict between generosity and greed, as in the movie *It's a Wonderful Life*.

The purpose of the setting, or why the author chose a tropical island over a major metropolitan city, for example, relates to another important element of literature—plot—or the plan of the story.

Plot

Plot is more than a series of events; plot is the plan or the arrangement of the story. A plot must contain a *cause/effect* relationship. Recall the example from the program:

A woman died and then her husband died.

This sentence provides a description of events in the order in which they happened, but it does not include causality. There is no plot.

A woman died and then her husband died of sorrow.

In this sentence information has been added which establishes a *cause/effect* relationship. Now there is a plot.

This sentence also suggests a *conflict*: the husband's natural will to live comes into conflict with his sorrow. Conflict can occur in several ways. Conflict can exist within individuals on a psychological or an emotional level as in the example cited above; conflict can also exist between individuals, between groups of people, and between an individual and forces of society or the environment.

The chief character faced with a conflict in a story is the *protagonist*. Whoever or whatever opposes the protagonist is the *antagonist*. In *The Wizard of Oz*, for example, Dorothy, who represents good, is the protagonist, and must face the force of evil, the

Wicked Witch of the West, the antagonist. In the film *It's a Wonderful Life* the protagonist George Bailey must fight the antagonist Mr. Potter who represents greed.

A plot line is made up of events that describe a specific conflict and the outcome.

PLOT LINE:

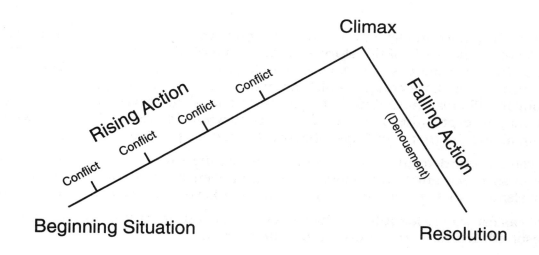

Soon after conflict is introduced, the author complicates the story with more incidents which contribute to the *rising action* of the plot. In *It's a Wonderful Life* the conflict between George Bailey and Mr. Potter is complicated by the death of George's brother, and finally by the uncle's loss of money. Tension builds in the story until it reaches the highest point or *climax*. You reach the climax or the point of highest tension when you start asking: "What will happen next? How will this turn out?" When you learn the outcome of the story—the climax has passed and you have reached the *falling action* or *denouement*. Here the author presents the solution or clarification of the plot.

If you choose to write an essay about plot, you must go beyond summarization. While it is important to identify the sequence of events, to write about plot you should relate the plot to other elements in the story. Ask yourself: How has the protagonist been changed by the events? Why are the events of the plot organized as they are? Remember, the object of writing about literature is to provide evidence for an interpretation. Retelling a story is not *interpreting* it.

Two techniques which may be used to reveal a plot are *flashback* and *foreshadowing*. Not all authors arrange the events in their stories chronologically. An author may use *flashback* by beginning the story with the conclusion and then working back. The film *It's a Wonderful Life* begins with George's crisis and *flashes back* to his childhood. The viewer learns a lot about George Bailey as a child and in this way learns of the events leading to his crisis.

Another technique, *foreshadowing*, provides hints about the outcome of a story. You may find foreshadowing throughout a narrative. This technique is used in Gail Godwin's short story, "Dream Children":

The worst thing. Such a terrible thing to happen to a young woman. It's a wonder she didn't go mad.

You are left wondering what terrible thing has happened to this woman. You don't know what to expect, but you do know to expect something strange or unusual.

Theme

The most important element in any literary work is the theme—the central point of the work. All other elements of the story—character, point of view, setting—advance this central idea. But the theme isn't always easy to identify. Cliches such as "What goes around comes around" or "Love conquers all" rarely describe an author's intentions. Just as you and your friends may have different interpretations of the movie you saw last night, each reader may interpret the theme of a story somewhat differently. Critics have been disagreeing about the theme of Shakespeare's *Hamlet* for hundreds of years!

As you do your detective work, you may find that there is more than one theme in a work. Theme is so important to any literary work that even if you base your essay on another literary element such as character, you should first have some idea of the work's theme.

The easiest way to identify the theme is to look carefully at the story's conflict and how it is resolved. Examine the one-sentence story again:

A woman died and then her husband died of sorrow.

The theme in this example probably centers around the husband's death. How and why did he die? Depending on the details of the story, the theme could be: "To love too deeply is a weakness" or "Courage, not love, is required to survive life's tragedies."

After deciding on a possible theme, go back and check specific details of the story, looking for possible contradictions. You may need to rework your statement of theme several times before you can identify the overall purpose controlling the story. For example, if you find that the husband was upset because his wife had willed her fortune to charity, you would have to rethink your statement, "To love too deeply is a weakness."

A valid interpretation of a work requires supporting evidence from the story. Look for specific examples in the text to help prove your thesis. In the program the student had to identify another theme for J. D. Salinger's *The Catcher in the Rye* when she discovered contradictions. The theme could not have been based on Phoebe's comment, "You don't like anything that's happening," because the student was able to find a number of things that Holden Caulfield *did* like. He liked the music of carousels, he liked his brother Allie, and he liked talking to Phoebe.

> *Remember*: Provide adequate evidence to support your interpretation. Without evidence, your interpretation has no value.

Understanding Poetry

The larger elements of literature—character, point of view, setting, plot and theme—are relevant in discussions of longer works such as novels, plays and short stories. Analyses of poems, however, require attention to other elements.

Poetry is the most condensed and concentrated form of literature. Poetry communicates the most in the least number of words. A good way to begin looking at poetry is to concentrate on its language.

Imagery

An image is the picture an author is able to create in the mind of the reader through words. As you saw in the program very different images come to mind when you read "cotton candy," "roller coaster," "hot dogs," and "sawdust" compared to "leaky faucet," "cracked plaster," "bare light bulb," and "a For Sale sign."

Images contribute to a poem's vividness; they can promote a sense of approval or disapproval; they can set a mood. Writers develop images that relate to characters or themes, and they can appeal to any one of the senses—sight, sound, touch, smell, taste—to evoke those images. If an author does her job, the reader begins to participate in the event of the poem by creating pictures in his or her mind. Tennyson's poem, "The Eagle," is built almost entirely around images.

THE EAGLE

By Alfred Lord Tennyson

He clasps the crag with crooked hands;
Close to the sun in lonely lands,
Ringed with the azure world, he stands.

The wrinkled sea beneath him crawls;
He watches from his mountain walls,
And like a thunderbolt he falls.

Figurative Language

With the use of imagery a writer causes our imaginations to participate in an event by producing pictures in our minds. Some of the same processes are at work when a writer uses figurative language. The use of figurative language requires you to make your own connections. Instead of saying that something is *very* American or *typically* American, you can compare it to something *known to be American*—baseball or apple pie, for instance. On the surface the words seem unrelated, but on a deeper level the reader makes the connection.

One type of comparison is the *simile*. A simile compares two unrelated objects using the words *like* or *as*. For example, "He is as American as apple pie." Recall the simile that appeared in the last line of "The Eagle":

And like a thunderbolt he falls.

Another type of figurative language is the *metaphor.* A metaphor compares one thing to another without using the words *like* or *as*. It is an implied comparison. We often use metaphors in everyday language, for example, "She's an angel," or "That book is a bomb."

A metaphor can be expressed in a phrase or as an entire story. In William Faulkner's short story, "A Rose For Emily," a woman poisons her lover and keeps his body in a room in her house. On a literal level this is an interesting story of a woman and her lover. On another level the entire story may be interpreted as a metaphor for the decline of the South after the Civil War.

Symbolism

Another way writers give their works deeper levels of meaning is through the use of *symbolism*. A symbol is anything that stands for something else. A rose symbolizes love. Water often represents the idea of eternal life. Most people associate serpents with Satan or evil. As with the other techniques of literature, you may need to dig deeper into a work to discover the symbols; authors often use them with subtlety. If a particular object, action or character is mentioned repeatedly, you can test its possible use as a symbol by looking for additional meaning.

As You Begin to Write

As you become more practiced at analyzing and interpreting literature, you will begin to notice all of these elements more readily. Use them when writing your interpretations. Listed below are some additional suggestions to keep in mind as you put your interpretation into writing:

- ▶ Include the name of the literary work and the name of the author in the first paragraph.

- ▶ Provide enough information about the work to show your readers you know what you are writing about—but avoid plot summary.

- ▶ Use literary present tense. The work may have been written in the past, but in a sense, it is always in the present. For example, we say that Huck Finn is a backwoods boy, not that he *was*.

- ▶ Refer to specific details in the work to provide evidence for your thesis. It is important to show how your evidence develops your thesis.

By gaining practice in writing about literature, you will develop more sophisticated interpretations of stories and poems. In this way you will not only learn about literature, you will also develop critical thinking/reading skills which will transfer to any subject you wish to master.

✔ Self Test

From the following list, select the word or phrase that most closely matches each statement below:

conflict	plot	imagery	interpretation
flashback	metaphor	antagonist	falling action (denouement)
supports	protagonist	foreshadowing	condensed (concentrated)
theme		symbol	first paragraph

1. _____ is a technique which gives readers details about an earlier event.

2. The chief character faced with a conflict is called the _____.

3. The _____ is made up of events that describe a specific conflict and its outcome.

4. As soon as the climax of the story is passed, the _____ begins.

5. Whoever or whatever represents the conflict in a story is the _____.

6. All other elements of a literary work—character, point of view, setting, plot—are utilized for one purpose: to express a _____.

7. The easiest way to identify the theme of a literary work is to look carefully at the _____.

8. Poetry is the most _____ and _____ form of literature.

9. Having a valid interpretation means citing specific evidence in the story which _____ your interpretation.

10. _____ causes our imaginations to produce pictures in our minds.

11. A _____ stands for something else and means more than what it is.

12. A _____ is an implied comparison.

13. When writing about a work of literature, you should include the author and the work in the _____.

14. _____ gives readers hints about the outcome of a story.

15. The object of writing about literature is to provide evidence for an _____.

Writing Assignments

1. Each line in Tennyson's poem, "The Eagle," contains imagery. Write one page (approximately 250 words) in which you identify the images (and any other poetic devices) and explain how they add to the total effect of the poem.

THE EAGLE

He clasps the crag with crooked hands;
Close to the sun in lonely lands,
Ringed with the azure world, he stands.

The wrinkled sea beneath him crawls;
He watches from his mountain walls,
And like a thunderbolt he falls.

2. Pick-a well-known children's story and explain the plot line. Include a discussion of the beginning situation, the complicating events, the conflict, the climax and the denouement.

Possible stories:

    The Good Samaritan
    Little Red Riding Hood
    Goldilocks and the Three Bears
    Jack and the Beanstalk
    Cinderella
    The Three Little Pigs

Answer Key

1. flashback
2. protagonist
3. plot
4. falling action or denouement
5. antagonist
6. theme
7. conflict
8. condensed, concentrated
9. supports
10. imagery
11. symbol
12. metaphor
13. first paragraph
14. foreshadowing
15. interpretation

APPENDIX

Transitions

Transitions, or connective phrases, are words and phrases which link or bridge sentences or independent clauses together. They <u>signal</u> the logic of related thoughts.

Illustration
introduces a particular case or concrete proof of a generalization

for example
for instance
in fact
thus
to illustrate
to demonstrate
specifically
in other words
namely
in particular

Summary or Conclusion
implies the end is approaching

in brief
indeed
in other words
therefore
thus
to summarize
in summary
in short
in conclusion
to conclude
finally
on the whole

Cause & Effect
shows logical result of what has gone before or said previously

accordingly
as a result
as a result of
consequently
as a consequence
hence
then
therefore
thereupon
thus
because
because of
for that reason
thereafter
according to
at this point

Contrast
introduces opposite side of case already stated

after all
although
and yet
apart from
conversely
despite
however
in contrast
in contrast to
instead
instead of
nevertheless
notwithstanding
on the contrary

Additions
continue previous thought in new sentence

again
* also
* beside
* besides
* equally
finally
furthermore
in addition
like
likewise
moreover
next
* similarly
too
as well as
* in like manner
* in the same way

* can be used in comparison

Time
orders chronology of
events

meanwhile
next
then
immediately
later
soon
in the meantime
afterward
at length
now
simultaneously
at the same time
subsequently
always
as soon as
at last
briefly
finally

on the other hand
otherwise
still
while
yet
nonetheless
even so
in spite of
even though

NOTES

NOTES

NOTES

NOTES

NOTES

NOTES

NOTES

NOTES